BE A MAN

THE BASICS OF BIBLICAL MANHOOD

JOHN PAUL BASHAM, GENERAL EDITOR

LifeWay Press®
Nashville, Tennessee

ISBN: 9781430060666
Item: 006104406

Dewey decimal classification: 248.4
Subject headings: RELIGION / CHRISTIAN MINISTRY / YOUTH

To order additional copies of this resource, write to LifeWay Resources Customer Service; One LifeWay Plaza; Nashville, TN 37234-0113; fax 615.251.5933; phone toll free 800.458.2772; order online at *www.lifeway.com;* email *orderentry@lifeway.com;* or visit the LifeWay Christian Store serving you.

Printed in the United States of America.
Student Ministry Publishing
LifeWay Resources
One LifeWay Plaza
Nashville, TN 37234

CONTENTS

A NOTE FROM THE EDITOR

We live in a culture where the bar has been set incredibly low for young men. Given the rampant problem of fatherlessness and our culture's lack of clarity on what it even means to be a man, it seems that we don't expect much from guys these days.

In contrast, Scripture calls men to fiercely pursue Christ and to be leaders in their homes, communities, and churches. This book is not a comprehensive or fool proof plan for the discipleship of young men; it is a spring board, a first step in the process of raising the bar for what we expect of young men. Whatever you do, don't read this book by yourself. Read it, share it, discuss it. If you are a student leader, read through it with a small group of young men. If you are a student, discuss it with a mentor and look for other guys who will join you in raising the bar on manhood.

My prayer for you as you read this book is that God would spark in you a determination to raise the bar for yourself and the young men around you. Don't be content to be a boy—to merely get by or stay out of trouble. Be a man. Humble yourself before God, determine both to be a disciple of Christ and to make disciples. Join me in praying that God would make men out of boys, and that He would raise up young men who will take up their cross and live on mission for Christ.

JOHN PAUL BASHAM

HOW TO GET THE MOST FROM THIS STUDY

1. READ EACH CHAPTER.
» Participate in the group discussions.

2. JOURNAL YOUR RESPONSES TO THE DISCUSSION QUESTIONS AT THE END OF EACH CHAPTER.
» Look up key Bible passages and meditate on the truth of these verses.
» Ask God to shape your understanding of both discipleship and manhood.
» Discuss your answers with a close friend or mentor.
» Apply the principles.

3. START A DISCIPLESHIP GROUP.
» Recruit a small group of guys to read through the book together and meet periodically to discuss each chapter.
» *Be a Man* has 7 chapters with three components of personal study for each. Most groups will do this study over the course of 7 weeks, but if your group follows a different schedule, that's OK.
» Don't rush. Allow time for the Spirit of God to work in you through His Word.

INTRO

ABOUT THE AUTHOR

John Paul Basham is the Manager of LifeWay Student Ministry Publishing. He served in the local church for 10 years before coming on staff at LifeWay and has a deep passion for the work of the church and its mission to make disciples. He is married to Crystal and has two boys, Levi and Titus.

What does it mean to be a man? The world offers a wide range of definitions for manhood, all biased in one direction or another, seemingly neglecting some or every part of the biblical definition of manhood. I can vividly remember milestone moments throughout my childhood and adolescence where my parents, church leaders, and mentors in the faith guided and instructed me in what it means to be a man.

One of the most impactful experiences of my young life was the first time I remember seeing my dad cry. Growing up, my father was always loving and caring, but he was tough, in charge, and commanded respect from all around him. My brother and I talk often about the time our dad finally decided he was tired of telling my older brother to stop riding his skateboard. My brother was always coming home all scraped up from falling off his board. One day he came home with a broken collar bone from a bad fall. My dad calmly picked up my brother's skateboard and broke it in half over his knee! I don't know if you've ever tried to break a nice skateboard, but they are built to withstand some serious damage, and my dad snapped it like a twig! There were no threats, no harsh words, simply a clear declaration that his patience had reached its end and obedience was no longer optional.

On another occasion, Dad was pulling apart some pallets and slipped a disc in his back. I was sitting outside with the dog when I heard him let out a shout. He never shed a tear, but simply came and laid down beside me and asked me to go get Mom because he hurt himself. He promptly passed out from the pain. These displays of his unwavering nature in disciplining us and his "tough it out" attitude that seemed to power through any situation were always attributes I aspired to. However, seeing him cry was an aspect of manhood contrary to all I understood manhood to be.

I watched my dad manage billion dollar construction projects, serve our church, love his wife, and raise his children, but his tears were the first "weakness" I had witnessed in him. This was exactly the point of discussion at the Promise Keepers rally I attended with him in Atlanta. I don't remember who was speaking, but the main theme was how biblical manhood allows *and* requires men to grant themselves permission to feel emotions that the world would say are "weak."

At our core, we as men have a responsibility to be vulnerable before the Lord in declaration of our insufficiency. Scripture is clear about how God chooses to display His strength in our weaknesses (2 Cor. 12:9-10), and it is only through our weakness we can truly see God. In reality, the world offers no support, no solace, no grace, and no release for men that won't lead them down a path of further destruction. Satan is battling desperately for the total collapse of men. He knows if he can weaken the men of the world and deceive them into believing they must suppress their emotions, keep their struggles to themselves, and suffer quietly under the weight of their pride, they will eventually be rendered useless.

The humility God requires men to adopt before His throne is exactly the heart posture that empowers us to live for Christ and propels us to the greatest depths of His blessing. This study is all about the journey to creating the right posture in men. I have identified seven key aspects of discipleship essential for any young man who longs to grow in Christ and build His kingdom. It is my firm belief that when young men come together to pursue Christ through these areas of study and hold each other accountable to God's call, they will be transformed and made into worthy vessels for the work of the Lord.

BIBLICAL MANHOOD

There are many theories today about what it means to be a man. Many in our culture would have us believe that a man is to be passive and indecisive. Others kick against these notions and claim manhood is defined primarily by aggression and physical strength. Still others claim the very idea of manhood is nothing more than a social construction, which we are free to do away with entirely. In contrast to these contradictory views, the Bible presents us with a picture of manhood that is both strong and loving, where men lead boldly yet serve with humility. In this chapter Chris White cuts through the chaff to help us uncover ten essential characteristics of godly men.

THEOLOGY

When it comes to pursuing Christ, all too often, the task of theology—studying about God and growing in our knowledge of who He is—gets overlooked. If we hope to gain any traction on the path of discipleship, we must progress beyond a mere surface-level understanding of God. In this chapter, Andy McLean demonstrates how every man who desires to truly follow Jesus must recognize that theology informs our thinking, shapes our feelings, instructs our living, and when engaged humbly, moves us to worship. A robust, biblical, Christ-centered understanding of God provides the necessary foundation for discipleship, without which we will falter and eventually give up on our pursuit of Christ.

SPIRITUAL DISCIPLINE

The call to discipleship is not merely a call to adopt a certain lifestyle or live by a set of rules: discipleship is an ultimately an invitation into a relationship with a person. The call of discipleship is a call to live in relationship with and follow Jesus. But how do we do that? No one enters into a personal relationship with Jesus, the Creator, Sustainer, and Redeemer (Col. 1:15-20), and responds with disinterest. Those who have truly come to know Jesus by faith will long to know Him more. Thankfully, God has given us means of doing so such as Bible study, prayer, worship, and accountability. We call these items spiritual disciplines. In this chapter, Zac Etheridge discusses several of the essential practices God has given us to grow in our knowledge, understanding, and application of what it means to follow Christ.

PERSONAL HOLINESS

Having established what discipleship is, uncovered a biblical understanding of manhood, set theology as the foundation of manhood, and identified key disciplines Christ has given us to pursue Him, we now turn to the fruit of discipleship—holiness. All who pursue Christ will also pursue holiness (1 Pet. 1:13-16). In this chapter, Clayton King challenges young men to carefully consider the direction and destination of their lives and what actions they need to take to ensure the ultimate aim of their lives is Christlikeness (Eph. 4:15-16). As we seek to be Christlike men and to grow in holiness, we must also recognize the threat sin poses to obtaining our goal. King challenges us to hate, starve, and outsmart sin in hopes of living faithfully in the freedom Christ has won for us through His death and resurrection.

MISSION

God took on flesh and dwelt among us for a specific purpose. He came to earth to seek and save the lost, to give up His life as a ransom for many (Luke 19:10). The call to discipleship is a call to join in the mission of Jesus, to take up our crosses and join Him in His work of redemption. In this chapter, Mike Taylor unpacks the biblical components of mission and challenges men to position themselves to be used by God. Joining in the mission of God requires risk, but as White makes clear it is the only risk worth taking.

LEADERSHIP

The call to discipleship is a call to lead. Particularly for young men, following Christ means leading others by setting an example for them in faith, love, conduct, and purity (1 Tim. 4:12). In this chapter, Ben Trueblood distinguishes Christian leadership from that of the world, reminding us that the goal of Christian leadership is not to make much of ourselves, but to make much of Jesus. It is only when we understand the power of Christ's death and resurrection that we will be empowered and strengthened to lead like Jesus. Trueblood pleads with us to fill the leadership gap in our churches, families, and communities by influencing those around us to turn to Christ and follow Him.

DISCIPLE MAKING

Jesus took ordinary men and transformed them into world changers. Jesus' first disciples were fishermen, tax collectors, and political activists when He called them. When they died, they had become pastors, church planters, and martyrs. These men not only followed Jesus passionately, but they also multiplied themselves. They embraced Jesus' call to make disciples of all nations. In this chapter, Jeff Borton makes a biblical case for young men to both to be disciples and to disciple others.

As you walk through these 7 chapters, my desire is for you to be convinced of the need to passionately pursue each and every area of study, and for God to ignite in you a passion for the world around you to come to know Him.

CHAPTER 1

BIBLICAL MANHOOD

ABOUT THE AUTHOR

Chris White, *president and founder of Mobilizing Students, has spent more than 20 years as a student pastor, worship leader, and missions mobilizer. His heart for the nations and visionary leadership, combined with his love for students, enables him to guide Mobilizing Students toward its goal of launching students who share Christ and plant churches among the unreached.*

Chris is an MDiv graduate of Southwestern Baptist Theological Seminary, a husband, dad of two, passionate Christ-follower, Bama fan, and loves his bold-roasted organic coffee. He and his wife, Christy, and their two kids live in Nashville, Tennessee.

I love true stories that inspire. My favorite is *Braveheart*. The 1995 film starring Mel Gibson, chronicles the story of William Wallace, a young peasant boy in Scotland who watches the English torture his village and kill his parents. He grows up with a strong dislike for the English rulers and a desire for freedom from their tyranny. When he becomes a young man, the English revisit his village and kill his fiancé. With sheer fury and raw determination, he rises up and starts a movement. Against all odds, Wallace and those who rally to his cause fight to free Scotland from the tyrannical rule of the English once and for all. Many successful battles and a movement of thousands of Scots strikes fear into King Edward I. William Wallace seems unstoppable. However, Wallace is ultimately caught and publicly executed, but not before crying out the most memorable line from the entire movie: *"Freedom!"*[1]

The sight of Wallace's public execution lit a fire in the hearts of those who fought alongside him, and they ultimately rallied the masses to their cause, winning Scotland's freedom in 1328. He died for what he believed in, and that's gutsy and manly. Right? Of course it is, but are toughness and gritty determination really all it takes to be a man?

What does it mean to be a man? How does the Bible define manhood? Our culture has muddied the definition of manhood in many ways, but what does the Bible say about it, and what does it actually look like? How would you define godly manhood?

First, we must ask why we need a biblical view of manhood. Why can't we form our own opinions of what it means to be men?

The obvious reason is that, since God created man, God created man to do certain things and live a certain way. Therefore, it makes sense for us to discover God's view on what it means to be a man rather than the world's. So, let's explore ten characteristics of biblical manhood.

Godly Men . . .

1. FOLLOW HARD AFTER GOD.

Real men love Jesus. The godly man understands that there is only one God, as revealed through His Son Jesus (1 Cor. 8:6; Col. 1:15-17), and that all other "gods" are simply idols made by man (Ps. 96:5; Hab. 2:18; Rom. 1:18-25). Therefore, in awe of this all-powerful and personal God of heaven and earth, this man surrenders his entire life to God with complete allegiance. He gives himself to God's purposes and to the advancement of His kingdom on earth. This man never looks back, because his heart has been forgiven and set free to live the way God intended. *Freedom.* Nothing replaces a heart that is free.

So, the godly man has not only come to grips with the fact that he was made for God's glory (Isa. 43:7), but he has also discovered that walking with Christ is the deepest source of pleasure he will experience (1 Pet. 1:8-9). A man cannot be godly without the power of the Holy Spirit, who dwells within him. However, the godly man relies on the Spirit's guidance, constantly looking to Him for strength and wisdom. This man is willing to endure anything for Christ's sake. This is a man who follows wholeheartedly after God. As the Bible says of King David, he is "a man after [God's] own heart"(Acts 13:22, ESV). David was certainly not perfect. What made him a man after God's own heart was his desire for God above all else. Much like David, the godly man keeps God at the center of his life. God is his anchor and his refuge—he humbly pursues God at all costs. When he gets it wrong or makes terribly selfish mistakes, he humbles himself, admits his wrongdoing, and realigns his heart to God's heart.

2. LIVE AND DIE FOR WHAT MATTERS.

The godly man has centered his life on Christ, which means that his focus is not on the temporary, but the eternal. Therefore, his eyes are focused on God's kingdom and living with eternal impact. Superficial things like name brand clothes, cars, likes on social media, or taking the perfect selfie no longer deeply concern him. Instead, the godly man thinks about things that matter. He re-evaluates everything in his life through the lens of eternity.

He knows that what the typical man chases after, what he used to chase after, will burn in the end (1 John 2:15-17). Godly men realize that worldly pursuits are empty—they won't endure, but godly pursuits have eternal ramifications. Chasing after the right GPA, the right college, the right job, the right house, the right cars, the right investments, personal achievements, trophies, and whatever else the world comes up with is no longer his primary purpose. He knows that all these things will perish. He does his best in all God gives him to do because he knows God has gifted him with certain abilities. When a man of God acts, he acts with his heart locked on Christ. This way of life focuses on those things that are eternal: the Word of God (Isa. 40:8), the souls of men (John 6:51), and things done through faith in Jesus (Heb. 11:6).

So when he plays soccer, football, baseball, a musical instrument, or goes to work, he does it as if he's doing it for the Lord (Col. 3:23). God expects our best, and we glorify God when we use our gifts for Him. The godly man also experiences great pleasure when he displays God's glory through his gifts.

However, he plays knowing the real reason he's on the team is not for the fleeting glory of winning games, but to glorify God and point others to Christ.

So, the godly man lives life with the future in mind—God's glorious kingdom. That's his focus. His heartbeat. A godly man lives and is willing to die for his belief, like other Christ-followers throughout the ages, including many of Jesus' own disciples. And he is free in doing so because his focus is not blurred with numerous demands. He has a single-minded focus on what really matters.

3. UNDERSTAND AND RESPECT AUTHORITY.

The godly man respects authority and submits to it because he has already submitted to God. He understands that he has no rights, no demands, and no entitlements. He laid them all down when he took up his cross and surrendered to Christ (Luke 9:23). Therefore, he knows all worldly authorities have been put in place by God to provide safe boundaries, maintain order, and punish the disobedient (Rom. 13:1-7).

This means the godly man strives to be respectful to his parents, police officers, teachers, coaches, government officials, his employer, and anyone else in authority over him. Of course, he may be frustrated by those people, but remains respectful. Godly men can certainly plead their cases or express their concerns in a God-honoring way, but they should never use disrespect to get a point across. Disrespect is a characteristic that belongs to a lost man—one not yet redeemed from his depraved heart of rebellion. The lost man is selfish, but the godly man seeks to be the opposite. The godly man is selfless, humble, and kind; he's not a pushover, but firm, rock-solid, and God-honoring.

Take Joseph for example. The Bible describes him as a handsome, well-built young man (Gen. 39:6). In Genesis 39, his boss' wife took notice of him and tried to entice him to sleep with her. He refused her, like a God-honoring man should, and ran out of the room. Yet, because his refusal embarrassed her, she accused him of acting inappropriately toward her. She lied to her husband and had Joseph thrown into prison. He sat in prison for two years for something he didn't do. He sat there without being disrespectful to his boss, without demanding his release, and without whining about his situation. Joseph trusted God. He knew all authorities on earth, even those who didn't honor God, were still subject to Him and under His control. Joseph knew God could make anything happen, so he trusted God's plan, even though he didn't understand it.

God used those two years to humble and prepare Joseph. Let's face it—Joseph was Jacob's favorite child. He needed to be taken down a few notches. After a few years and two correctly interpreted dreams, Pharaoh called on Joseph to interpret his own dream. The interpretation and Joseph's plan to fight the famine pleased Pharaoh, so Pharaoh exalted Joseph to the highest authority in Egypt, second only to Pharaoh himself. So, God's plan came to pass, and Joseph grew through the experience and learned to submit to authority. As a result, he became an authority in Egypt, saved Egypt and his family from starvation, and was reunited with his family after years of separation.

Joseph demonstrated the way a godly man should view authority. The godly man remembers that all authority in heaven and earth has been given to Christ (Matt. 28:18), and Christ has placed all authorities, rulers, and governments in their place (Rom. 13:1-7). So, "Humble yourselves before the Lord, and He will lift you up" (Jas. 4:10, NIV).

4. STAND FOR TRUTH.

The godly man takes a stand for truth. However, in order to stand for truth, you must know what truth is. Jesus makes it very clear in Scripture that He is truth. Jesus said, "I am the way, the truth, and the life. No one comes to the Father except through me" (John 14:6). This means that Truth is not a concept, but a person—Jesus Christ. So, to take a stand for truth in our world means you take a stand for the things that matter to Jesus. The Bible makes it clear that all things were made by the Son, through the Son, and for the Son (John 1:1-3; Col. 1:15-17). We also know that He was with God in the beginning because Genesis says, "Let Us make man in Our image" (1:26). "Us" and "Our" refers to the Father, Son (Jesus), and Holy Spirit—what we call the *Trinity*. The Son was not only present at creation, but along with the Father and Holy Spirit, spoke the entire world into existence. Therefore, the entire Bible from beginning to end is about Jesus. It's Jesus' breath on paper, His spoken Word, and it is all 100 percent true.

So, for the godly man, Truth is a person. If we know Christ, we must stand for Truth—we must stand for Him. This means at the very least that we put away falsehood or lies and simply tell the truth. No more fronts or deception. No more pretending to be something we're not—we just tell the cold hard truth. When we tell the truth, we may have to face the consequences, but our honesty will demand the respect of others and make us trustworthy men of integrity. People are hungry for someone they can trust.

Being godly men also means we stand up for things that Jesus stands up for in His Word: the poor, the weak, the homeless, the abused, the trafficked, the widow, the orphan, the unborn, for the life of all mankind, and a million other things. We must know His Word in order to know what to stand for. Even if your voice is the only voice in the room taking a stand, a godly man will stand up for the truth no matter what.

Jesus stood up for the woman caught in adultery when the crowds wanted to stone her for her sin (John 8:7). Her life was spared and changed, and Jesus' words challenged the crowd to think about their own lives. When we stand up for truth, others will be challenged to consider their own lives as well.

Before the reformation in the 1500s, the only people who had copies of the Bible were the Catholic priests, and the scribes who took care of the scrolls. No one could check what the priests said against Scripture because personal copies of the Bible weren't available. During the protestant reformation, an English scholar and reformer named William Tyndale thought all people should be able to read the Bible. So, at great risk to his life, Tyndale translated the Bible from Latin into English—the first copy for the common man. The church leaders saw this as a challenge to their power and captured him. He was strangled and burned alive at the stake in 1536.[2] Thanks to his willingness to take a stand or the truth and ultimately die for it, we now have copies of the Bible in our language, in our homes, and on our phones and tablets.

The godly man models his life after Christ, so the truth is worth taking a stand for truth, no matter the cost. Isaiah 7:9b says, "If you do not stand firm in your faith, then you will not stand at all." It's hard to be the only one standing for truth; however, I assure you that you are never alone, though sometimes it may feel like you are. So, stand and be unashamed!

5. RESPECT AND HONOR WOMEN.

Godly men see women as God sees them—human beings with souls, who will live forever, and have been made in the image of God (Gen. 1:27; 1 Pet. 3:7). Like us, they were made to bring God glory. It is important to note that we live in a culture that constantly degrades and objectifies women. How do we view women from God's perspective in our over-sexualized culture with instant access to pornography? Honestly, holding this view is difficult, we need to be aware that temptations to see women as objects for our pleasure are all around us, even for grown, married men. I know this is a very real and sensitive topic, but one that we must discuss because women are daily being destroyed by disrespect and dishonor. We need a truthful, honest, and plain approach to embracing a godly view of women.

When God said, "Let Us make man in Our image" (Gen. 1:26), the word "man" refers to mankind or humanity, which includes both men and women.[3] Therefore, men and women were both made in God's image, to bring glory to His name. Thinking of women in any other way reduces them to something less than what God intended them to be, and this offends Him.

Satan would have us see women as objects to be used for our personal pleasure because his mission is to steal, kill, and destroy (John 10:10). He will use all sorts of tactics to deceive us and distort the truth. From the beginning, Satan has told all kinds of lies. The Bible tells us that Satan is not just any liar, but the father of all lies (John 8:44). So, it would make sense for him, as the current and temporary ruler of this age, to lie to us about who women really are. He tells us that women are more like possessions than people—things to be desired, used, and discarded. When we believe these lies, we not only open ourselves up to sexual temptation, but we also damage the women in our lives by encouraging them to embrace these lies as well. When men and women buy into these lies, they completely miss God's design for marriage. God intended for us to glorify Him inside a marriage that shares life-long intimacy, companionship at the deepest level, and guilt-free sexual oneness.

Another way many are living out this lie is through pornography. According to a recent study, 67 percent of guys and 49 percent of girls say viewing pornography on a regular basis is acceptable.[4] Let me warn you here, if you watch porn, you are a direct contributor to the enslavement of women and children and are creating a higher demand for sex trafficking all over the world. Don't believe what you see on the Internet. These women do not enjoy what they're doing; very few women are in the porn industry for the money, the rest are being trafficked.[5] Most porn is scripted by men and for men. It's not real, meaning: this is not truly how a woman desires to be treated. Engaging in pornography is pure idolatry—worshiping what has been created, rather than the Creator (Rom. 1:25). Again, when we view pornography, we believe the Enemy's lies about women. Satan always tempts us to meet a legitimate need in an illegitimate way that dishonors God and robs us of dignity. The world's way is cheap, quick, unsatisfying, destructive, and selfish.

A godly man honors women at all times (1 Cor. 13:4-8; 1 Pet. 3:7). He treats them with dignity and respect, as highly valued, precious, and beautiful. He insures they are not mistreated, he sacrifices himself for them (Eph. 5:25), and he prays for God's strength to remain pure in his dating relationships. It's time for godly men to rise up, take a stand, and be the gentlemen God has created us to be.

6. PROTECT AND PROVIDE.

God calls men to provide for and protect their families. God has made men the head of the household, just like Christ is the head of the church (1 Cor. 11:3). Therefore, the man is to lead and do for his family what Christ does for him. In Genesis 3, when Adam and Eve disobeyed God, they immediately hid from Him.

Our natural response when we do something wrong is to hide or cover it up. It's impossible to hide from God. When God came to look for them in the garden, whom did He call out to? Eve? Nope. Genesis 3:9 says "So the LORD God called out to the man and said to him, 'Where are you?'" That's right. He called to the man, not the woman. Why? He holds the man responsible for his wife and his family. Now, God knew where Adam was. He asked the question because he wanted Adam to acknowledge where he was—hiding in disobedience. He wanted Adam to be a man and own up to his sin. Instead, Adam blamed his wife, who then blamed the serpent. God, in His love, performed the first blood sacrifice by killing an animal, taking its skin, and using it to cover over their nakedness. He then cursed the serpent and the ground and punished Adam and Eve by removing them from His garden. There are real consequences for disobedience to God. Blood was required for the covering of sin for Adam and Eve and for us. Eventually, Jesus would cover all believers by the shedding of His own blood for the sins of the world.

So, one of man's God-given roles is to protect his family. Adam didn't do that. He allowed his wife to be led astray by the Enemy, and we've all suffered the curse of that sin ever since. In that single moment of negligence and disobedience, all of humanity was plunged into darkness and separation from God.

God had also provided everything Adam and Eve needed in the garden. Yet, after their disobedience, God removed them from the garden and told Adam, "You will eat bread by the sweat of your brow until you return to the ground, since you were taken from it. For you are dust, and you will return to dust" (Gen. 3:19). From that point on, Adam had to provide for his family by working the land. Instead of having all he needed provided for him, he had to provide.

You see, when we buy the Devil's lie and ignore what God has told us to do, we suffer long-term consequences that cause more pain than we ever intended. Someone once said that sin will take you farther than you wanted to go, cost you more than you wanted to pay, and keep you longer than you wanted to stay. One of the primary roles godly men must fill is to protect and provide. By doing so, we create an environment where we can be the spiritual leaders of our future wives and families that God created us to be (Eph. 5:25-33).

7. SERVE OTHERS.

Godly men follow Jesus' example and serve others without being asked. Paul instructed believers to "do nothing out of rivalry or conceit, but in humility consider others as more important than yourselves. Everyone should look out not only for his own interests, but also for the interests of others" (Phil. 2:3-4). Jesus also taught that the very reason He came was not to be served, but to serve (Mark 10:45). If men claim to be true followers of Christ, then we must become like Christ in His nature and character. We must imitate His life and the way He treated others. He served others in countless ways, ultimately serving all of humanity by His sinless life, sacrificial death and resurrection, and His offer of forgiveness and salvation.

Jesus was the ultimate man, the fullness of God's deity in bodily form, the all-powerful, all-loving, all-knowing, sovereign God of the universe. Yet, He chose to serve, rather than demand everyone to serve Him. In reality, He had every right to demand that, yet even on the night before His death, He got down on His knees and washed His disciples feet (John 13:1-17)—something a house servant would normally do.

Since Jesus was the ultimate man, and we are striving to be more like Him, then we must commit ourselves to serving others. Remember, we also have this encouragement from Jesus Himself, "'Whatever you did for one of the least of these brothers of Mine, you did for Me'" (Matt. 25:40). Serve your parents, your teachers, your coaches, your friends, and your church. Not because they deserve it or even demand it; serve because you love Jesus. Serving others provides us opportunities to identify with and honor Christ by following His example. His servant heart should become your heart. That's what godly men pursue.

8. SHOW COMPASSION.

The godly man hates injustice so much that he does something about it. He shows compassion toward those who are lost, mistreated, abused, helpless, hopeless, weak, and needy. What does that look like? Well, maybe it looks like pulling over to help someone change a tire. Maybe it's giving up your seat in a crowded room for a lady who's standing. Maybe it's looking past the anger of a bully to a heart that desperately needs Jesus, and stepping up to share the hope of Christ with him. Maybe it's protecting someone who can't protect himself. Or, it may be that God breaks your heart for a people group or nation that hasn't heard about Christ and you move there as a missionary so they can hear the gospel.

Jesus had compassion on a crowd of four thousand when He chose to feed them after they had followed Him for three days (Matt. 15:32). Jesus showed compassion on the woman caught in adultery, when he healed the sick, the lame, the blind, or the demon-possessed. He lived a life of compassion—it was His nature. This ultimately took Him to the cross, where He laid down His life for you and me. As Jesus said, "No one has greater love than this, that someone would lay down his life for his friends" (John 15:13).

If we are to be godly men, we must be real men who aren't afraid to cry, make sacrifices, show compassion for others, or be the answer to problems we see. We must lead the way in being men of compassion. Remember, real men are godly men, and godly men are like Jesus.

9. MAKE HARD CHOICES

The godly man makes hard choices even when it hurts. When I first got married, our house was broken into and ransacked. My wife was terrified by the experience, and even to this day we wake up at the slightest sound. An experience like that just changes you. The horrible thing about this experience was that the person who broke into our house and robbed us was our spiritual mentor's oldest son, a young man I had given up many Saturdays to counsel. He was a troubled kid, and as a young student pastor, I tried to help him. Yet, he betrayed us and robbed us.

When we eventually discovered he was the one who robbed us, we were faced with the choice of pressing charges. This guy had been in and out of trouble, but his parents always bailed him out, which was part of the problem. We were living in Florida at the time, which has a law that states any crime where the assailant goes in or out with guns is considered a felony with a two-year minimum prison sentence. Well, he had stolen all my shotguns and rifles and fled with them, making it a felony if I pressed charges. The police continued asking me to make a decision on whether or not I wanted to press charges. So, I was faced with a choice that boiled down to me either letting him get away with a felony or sending him to prison. I had knots in my stomach. How could I send my mentor's son to prison? After agonizing over it, talking with some other spiritual mentors, and lots of prayer, I decided to press charges. He went to prison, and my mentors didn't speak to me for years. The decision and consequences really hurt, but I knew it was the right thing to do. If it had been anyone else I wouldn't have blinked about pressing charges, yet because I knew this young man, I was tempted to let him off easy; however, I knew that if I did, he would miss out on a critical lesson he needed to learn.

Although we ultimately did the difficult and right thing, it was hard to be mistreated by our mentors for making that decision. Yet, three years later, our mentors came to us in tears and asked for our forgiveness. They admitted that they were wrong for the way they responded. They said they knew we did the right thing, but that they couldn't be our friends at the time because they had lost their son. We were able to make amends, and the respect they have for us now has increased tremendously because of that experience.

There were many times people tried to deter Jesus from going to the cross, including His own disciples. Even Jesus felt the temptation to avoid going to the cross; still, His response was, "But that is why I came to this hour" (John 12:27). In Luke 9:51, the Bible says, "When the days were coming to a close for Him to be taken up, He determined to journey to Jerusalem." Jesus made the hard decision to lay down His life, and He would not be deterred for any reason—too much was at stake.

Godly men make hard choices—even when it hurts, is inconvenient, or others don't agree—simply because it's the right thing to do. We must be men who do the right thing and make the hard choices along the way, so that others may benefit and we may follow in Christ's footsteps.

10. FINISH!

The godly man finishes what he starts. He keeps his promises and follows through because God keeps every promise He makes to us (2 Cor. 1:20; 2 Peter 1:3-4). This generation is full of starters, and what we need is for people to finish what they start. About half of marriages in the United States end in divorce.[6] And sadly, some studies have shown that divorce rates among professing Christians aren't much better.[7] However, it is also true that those who say they keep God at the center of their marriages struggle less and have lower rates of divorce.[8] If only we could finish what we start and be men of integrity. Finish the game. Finish the season. Finish the course. Finish the task of taking the gospel to the nations so the whole world may know the hope we have in Christ.

If Jesus had approached the cross the way we approach the tough parts of relationships, sports, or life, He would've given up and we would all be headed to eternal separation from Him in hell. You see how costly it is to quit. Godly men don't quit. They get knocked down but get right back up. They get mistreated but press on. They get discouraged but keep their eyes on Jesus and finish what they start. We must be men of faith who embody the character of Christ and persevere to the end. You've probably heard it said that "quitters never win and winners never quit." It's true. We are known far more by what we overcome than what we accomplish. Take heart, for Jesus has already overcome the world (John 16:33). So finish! It's what the godly man does.

As we examine our lives through the lens of these ten characteristics of a godly man, it can be overwhelming to try to be all these things. So don't try. Let's keep in mind that these things are not a list to be performed, but are supernaturally produced from the overflow the Holy Spirit in you. He guides you and empowers you to be more like Christ, our ultimate example. When you submit to God as a believer, remain in His Word daily, and continue in obedience to His commands, these things will flow freely from your life. They are not easy by any stretch, but you will find yourself being shaped into the man God intended you to be as the Holy Spirit empowers you on your journey.

QUESTIONS FOR DISCUSSION

1. What characteristics come to mind when you think of being a godly man?

2. Name some examples of godly men in your life. How can you learn from these men?

3. What things need to change in your own life in order for you to grow in godliness?

4. What things do you struggle with that could keep you from being a godly man?

5. How can you eliminate the barriers that stand in your way of becoming more of a godly man?

6. Do you think others would describe you as a godly man? Why or why not?

7. What would people say is missing or lacking in your ability to live out godly manhood?

8. What would you say are the benefits of becoming a godly man?

9. Do you think it's worth it to live God's way? What about the world's way?

10. Are you willing to do whatever it takes to become a godly man? Discuss the changes you plan to make.

CHAPTER 2
THEOLOGY

ABOUT THE AUTHOR

Andy McLean *serves as the editor for The Gospel Project for Students, and is the author of* Big Questions: Developing a Christ-Centered Apologetic. *A life-long learner in the areas of theology and apologetics, Andy has earned a Bachelor of Arts (B. A.) in religion, a Master of Divinity (MDiv) in Christian Apologetics, a Master of Arts (M. A.) in Science and Religion, a Master of Theology (Th. M) in Philosophy of Religion, and is currently working toward a Ph. D in Systematic Theology. Andy and his wife, Sarah, have four children: Isaac, Caleb, Timothy, and Tobias.*

Discipleship is ultimately about becoming more like Jesus. All the things we do as Christians—prayer, service, missions—are never an end in themselves. We engage in these things in the hopes that they will help in our task of reflecting Jesus with our lives as we seek to make much of Him.

When it comes to discipleship, theology is often overlooked. For many, the path of discipleship consists of focusing on other aspects of the Christian life that bring us closer to Christ, such as those discussed in other chapters of this study. While those aspects are certainly necessary and help us become more like Christ, the discipline of theology is essential to each and every one of them. If we don't think carefully and deeply about what we believe about God, we will either give up on the prospect of following Christ altogether or set a course for discipleship that ultimately fails to gain traction.

If asked how important the role of theology is in their lives, most people will likely say theology has little to no value for them personally. For them, theology is an academic exercise or something only for super-spiritual believers. When ranked against everything else, theology would score near the bottom, or maybe even dead last.

What we often fail to realize is that every person is a theologian. We all *do* theology on some level. Even if we don't actively recognize this, we all live out our deeply held theological beliefs on a daily basis. Whether taking a stand on either side of the big debates like abortion or marriage, or maybe even considering a personal question like whether to get romantically involved with an unbeliever, our theology ultimately dictates our behavior.

Whether we realize it or not, theology is important, especially since our theological beliefs lie at the core of who we are as people. This is why A. W. Tozer once said, "What comes into our minds when we think about God is the most important thing about us."[1] For Tozer and countless others, the role of theology in discipleship is essential to becoming more like Christ.

When discussing how theology plays a vital role in our discipleship, it is important to first define what we mean by the term *theology*. While there are several ways to define theology, one simple way of describing the purpose of theology is this: to know God by the means He alone has provided so that we might live faithful lives in His service. In other words, there is a knowledge aspect to doing theology, consisting primarily of what we would call the biblical doctrines of the Christian faith and what these doctrines teach us about the Triune God. Additionally, this definition tells us that there is a method God has given us to learn these doctrines—studying Scripture. Finally, there is an end goal to theology—to live faithful and holy lives in obedience to God and to help others do the same.

What are some specific ways theology contributes to personal discipleship? How can studying theology, like the other topics discussed throughout this study, aid us in becoming more like Jesus in our daily lives?

THEOLOGY INFORMS OUR THINKING

One of the ways theology informs our thinking is by providing a foundation for knowing what we believe. Sadly, many professing Christians can't articulate what they believe or why they believe it. For them, being a Christian is just part of their culture—they grew up in the church, were raised by Christian parents, and simply adopted those beliefs as a result. They have never taken ownership of their faith or taken the time to carefully consider exactly what it is they claim to believe. As a result, these people are often negatively affected by the changing tides of the culture around them—believing one cultural trend after another instead of relying on the unchanging truth of God's Word.

Taking theology seriously, deeply understanding the Bible's major doctrines, provides an unshakable foundation in the midst of cultural confusion. It provides a holistic worldview that not only makes sense in itself, but also makes sense of the world around us. As C. S. Lewis once stated, "I believe in Christianity as I believe that the sun has risen, not only because I see it, but because by it I see everything else."[2] A Christian worldview comprised of sound theology is the lens that allows us to see this world from the right perspective.

For example, take the much-heated debate within American culture over the topic of abortion. Every opinion expressed on this issue comes from a person's worldview, and that person's worldview has beliefs regarding life at conception, the personhood of the fetus, and the rights of the mother. Of course, many of these worldviews and the beliefs associated with them lack a solid foundation. They are inconsistent, contradictory, or completely based on emotion with no rational support. However, in the Christian worldview, the position of being pro-life isn't based on faulty reasoning or emotions. Instead, the Christian perspective is rooted in the doctrine that all persons are created in the image of God and contain inherent dignity, value, and worth as a result. Without this theological foundation for the value of human life, the Christian view that abortion is wrong would just be another competing voice in a sea of voices without rational support.

Of course, theology not only gives us clarity with regard to the big topics and debates in our culture, but also sheds light on many other seemingly small things we encounter on a daily basis. Students today are faced with competing belief systems fighting for their allegiance. These much subtler worldviews often hide behind the guise of a movie, television series, or song lyrics, and as a result come at us in an indirect manner. Unless we are equipped to think critically and biblically about these messages, we will naturally absorb the worldviews these different mediums present.

By having a healthy dose of theology, you'll be able to spot the counterfeit when it comes across your path. You will only be able to recognize falsehood if you know the truth. In encouraging his young disciple, Timothy, to give attention to the Word and the faithful teaching of Scripture, Paul said, "Pay close attention to your life and your teaching; persevere in these things, for by doing this you will save both yourself and your hearers" (1 Tim. 4:16).

Theology also provides us with the content necessary to understand ourselves and the world we live in. Apart from a working knowledge of the Bible's major doctrines, the Christian who seeks to go further down the path of discipleship will meet roadblock after roadblock. We must allow the discipline of theology to inform our thinking.

THEOLOGY SHAPES OUR FEELINGS

Theology also helps us by giving shape to our emotions. In essence, theology helps us fulfill the greatest commandment. When asked what the greatest commandment was, Jesus responded by saying, "Love the Lord your God with all your heart, with all your soul, and with all your mind. This is the greatest and most important command" (Matt. 22:37-38). In essence, Jesus was commanding His followers to love God with all that they are and all that they have, to love God with all their being.

Too many Christians fall into the mindset that loving God is primarily an emotional act, something that only involves their affections. They wrongly assume that loving God is only a matter of the heart. However, according to Jesus' words, such thinking is clearly false. According to Him, we love God with our entire being, including both the heart and mind.

Loving God with our entire being protects us from being compartmentalized Christians who only love God with a portion of who we are. Our love for God directly corresponds with our knowledge of Him. In other words, our love for God deepens when our knowledge of God deepens.

Of course, you can know all sorts of things about God, or know a great deal of Christian theology, and still miss out on being in right relationship with Him (Jas. 2:19). That is a tragic possibility. However, it is still true that the more you know a person—let's say a friend or family member—the more you grow to love that person. The same is true about our relationship with God. The more we truly come to know Him—His character, His will, His love for us—the more we will love Him.

It is the desire of every person to be fully known and fully loved. We see this type of love demonstrated in the garden before the fall—both between God and humanity and the first married couple. It wasn't until after sin entered the human race that shame invaded our relationships (Gen. 3:7-11). With that shame came the tendency to cover and hide ourselves out of fear that if another person sees who we truly are, they will never be able to fully love us.

This is why we have convinced ourselves that in order to be fully loved we have to guard against being fully known by others. Yet, we also intuitively know that genuine love—the type of love that doesn't abandon—doesn't run when faced with the truth of who that person is. God fully loves us, while at the same time fully knowing us. When we seek to know Him by growing in our knowledge of Him and His character, our love for Him increases.

THEOLOGY INSTRUCTS OUR LIVING

Not only does theology inform our thinking and give shape to our emotions, but it instructs our living as well. As we have already mentioned, we must not compartmentalize the Christian life. We shouldn't fall into the trap of only feeling or thinking deeply about God—we are called to do both. Likewise, the Christian life can't be summed up as only knowing and loving God; it involves a way of living that reflects the relationship we have with Him.

The things we know about God through theology should not only impact the way we feel or think, but they should also impact the way we live. When we internalize the biblical teachings throughout Scripture, we begin to develop and live out a Christian worldview.

Biblical Manhood

Consider the topic of biblical manhood. For students today, the topic of manhood is littered with a variety of definitions and descriptions. One view the surrounding culture presents equates manhood as men being passive and indecisive, incapable of keeping pace both intellectually and verbally with their female counterparts. There are also many who kick against these trends and end up adopting hypermasculinity, or the practice of seeing manhood as primarily defined by physical strength, aggression, and sexual conquest. Another view of manhood our culture presents seeks to do away with all manliness. In fact, many within our culture would argue that the very ideas of manhood and womanhood are merely social constructions that can be ignored. For them, there is no difference between the sexes, and each person can determine their sexual identity aside from the biological parts they were born with.

In light of all this confusion, how should the Christian respond? How should we understand our own manhood, especially as it relates to living out God's design for our lives? It begins with knowing what the Bible says about the topic of manhood, starting in Genesis and working our way through Revelation. It involves having a biblical theology of manhood that not only recognize what is false about our culture's understanding, but also articulates the goodness found in God's unique design of men and women.

When turning to the Bible for this topic, we must begin where manhood, as designed by God, began—the garden of Eden. Even though the first two chapters of the Bible covered a massive amount of information, we can learn a great deal about what the Author of manhood originally had in mind when He designed the first man, Adam. We see what God designed man and woman for and that he declared them to be good. When God took the initiative to create Adam, His intention was to make him (and Eve) distinct from the rest of creation. They were to have a special place among creation because they would bear the image and likeness of God. This meant that they were to be co-stewards with God over the rest of creation, ruling over "the fish of the sea, the birds of the sky, the livestock, all the earth, and the creatures that crawl on the earth" (Gen. 1:26). Not only that, but they were also to reflect God in the way they related to one another, giving an earthly example of the intimate relationships that exist between the members of the Trinity—God the Father, Jesus the Son, and the Holy Spirit.

The Bible affirms that men and women, in terms of their worth and value, are wholly equal. Yet, while being equal, we see that God created men and women with different roles and functions in the garden. Adam was created and instructed by God to lead his wife, Eve, and the family they would one day have. Paul taught us that Christ loves the church and gave Himself up for her (Eph. 5:25). Adam was to demonstrate that same servant-leadership as originally designed by God. Adam had been graciously given the perfect example of fatherhood—God the Father. Adam was called to lead and shepherd his children in a way that reflected God's original design.

Even in the Bible's first two chapters we can see that manhood involves the ability to lead, guide, and protect. In fact, God called Adam out when he failed to take initiative in these areas. In Genesis chapter 3, we see that Adam was present when Eve was tempted by the serpent. Most people imagine that she was alone and Adam was off doing something else, but that isn't what the text says. The Bible says, "The woman saw that the tree was good for food and delightful to look at, and that it was desirable for obtaining wisdom. So she took some of its fruit and ate it; she also gave some to her husband, *who was with her*, and he ate it" (Gen. 3:6, emphasis mine). Not only that, but God also turned to Adam when addressing their collective sin and specifically called him out over his lack of leadership by saying, "Because you listened to your wife's voice and ate from the tree..." (Gen. 3:17).

Of course, this doesn't mean Eve didn't sin; it only shows that God went to Adam because of his God-given role of leading, guiding, and protecting the family. Even though we, like Adam, often fail in those God-designed roles today, we are still called to live out biblical manhood on a daily basis. Apart from the Bible giving us the biblical theology of what it means to be a man, we would be left in the dark as to the way God designed us and intends us to reflect Him as men.

You may be thinking, "I'm just in middle or high school. I'm not married, and I definitely don't have a family of my own. Can't this stuff wait?" The reality is that even now, as young Christian men, you are being shaped, molded, and equipped to one day become godly men, godly husbands, and godly fathers. Not only that, but leading, providing, and protecting others are only a few of the things God calls all men to do in carrying out their God-given roles as men. These aren't things that only apply to you when you reach a certain age. You should engage in and cultivate these practices even now in order to reflect the type of character we see in God throughout Scripture; the type of character that is tough and tender, strong and humble.

Our Identity in Christ

Another doctrine that informs the way we live is our identity as believers. It comes as no surprise that confusion over issues of identity partly stem from the cultural air we breathe. The vast majority of students tend to find their identity through labeling themselves. Students typically create these labels through certain skills or traits they deeply cherish. Maybe they label themselves as good students, skilled athletes, or as a part of the popular crowd.

The common denominator behind all of these is that students tend to find their identity horizontally in the things around them as opposed to vertically in a relationship with God. Take Paul's words to the church at Colossae as an example. He said, "God wanted to make known among the Gentiles the glorious wealth of this mystery, which is *Christ in you*, the hope of glory" (Col. 1:27, emphasis mine). The reality of Jesus in us carries tremendous implications for how believers should see ourselves. Once students are able to grasp the truth from Scripture, knowing that their identity is found in the One who created them and not in the created things around them, they will benefit from living in this reality.

Faith and Works

A third example of how theology shapes and informs our living can be seen in how people think about salvation. Because many people do not know the Bible's teaching very well, they end up adopting an unbiblical view of salvation. They deny that salvation is a gift of God's grace alone through faith in Christ alone. They feel the need to add to God's grace through their own effort or good works. Not only that, but many also reason that they can't truly be the recipients of God's grace until they first make an effort to clean up their act before coming to God. They assume that they must change their speech or quit bad habits in order to earn God's approval.

The idea that we must do certain things in order to attain salvation is clearly unbiblical (Eph. 2:8-9). We can never earn favor with God through our efforts, and no amount of good works can somehow cancel out the penalty that our sins justly deserve. We are all, as Paul said, guilty before God, and dead in our trespasses and sins (Eph. 2:1-3; Titus 3:4-7).

The Christian worldview is clear in that no amount of good works could ever secure our salvation (Rom. 11:5-6; Titus 3:4-7). While every other world religion involves an attempt to earn salvation through a series of works, Christianity is clear that salvation is a gift that is given to us by a loving and gracious God. As Paul said, "He [God] made the One [Jesus] who did not know sin to be sin for us, so that we might become the righteousness of God in Him [Jesus]" (2 Cor. 5:21). When we turn from our sins and submit to the lordship of Christ over our lives and place our trust and faith in Him alone, our sin is not only atoned for through the substitutionary sacrifice of Christ on our behalf, but His righteousness is also credited to our account, so that we might be in right relationship with God.

Where do good works come into the picture? Does the Christian doctrine of salvation eliminate doing good works altogether? Absolutely not. The biblical writers talked a great deal about what it means to live rightly before God and others. Paul, Peter, and John—among the others—went into great detail about the type of good works believers in Christ should display in their daily lives. However, the key is recognizing that good works are the response to grace at work in our lives, and not the cause of it. In other words, good deeds and works are the fruit of a relationship with Christ, not the root. If those are reversed, then what you are left with is a legalistic type of Christianity that seeks to win God's approval through human effort alone.

In this example you can see how important it is to be students of the Word, developing a biblical theology that informs our thinking, shapes our emotions, and influences the way we live on a daily basis. There are countless people in our culture striving to be better people and to live a better life, in the vain hope that they will one day be made right with God. They live by a list of do's and don'ts, thinking that if they live by these rules well enough, everything will turn out alright in the end. But that isn't the case. Only Christ has the power to change the heart, and it is only through His power that lives can be transformed as well.

God's Sovereignty

A final example of theology impacting the way we live is in the area of God's sovereignty. There are many things we could say on this topic, but in short, God's sovereignty refers to His control of all things. This doctrine can be an immense source of comfort and strength as you walk through dark and difficult times.

No one is immune to evil and suffering. Some of us experience it in a more direct way—a terminal diagnosis or the loss of a loved one. And some of us experience evil in an indirect way—we suffer as the result of the consequences of another person's sins. No matter how great or small our trials may seem, we all suffer on some level.

The Bible is well aware of this reality and has a great deal to say on the subject of evil and suffering. However, Christians throughout the centuries have endured such times of hardships knowing that God is good and is in control. He is not only in control during these times, but is also working all things together for the good of those who love Him and "are called according to His purpose" (Rom. 8:28).

Christian theology teaches us that we will all experience evil and suffering simply because we live in a broken and fallen world. However, Christian theology also equips us to endure these times and live in faithful and joyful obedience as we wait for the time when Christ will do away with all that is wrong with the world and make all things new. Apart from a biblical theology of suffering, the apostle Paul never would have been able to pen these words to the Corinthians: "Therefore we do not give up. Even though our outer person is being destroyed, our inner person is being renewed day by day. For our momentary light affliction is producing for us an absolutely incomparable eternal weight of glory. So we do not focus on what is seen, but on what is unseen. For what is seen is temporary, but what is unseen is eternal" (2 Cor. 4:16-18).

Other examples can be given to illustrate the important role that theology plays in instructing the way we live. However, while these things have an informational side to them, the goal of theology has always been to transform the way we live. That transformation only comes about as we take the time to internalize God's truth and hide it deep within our hearts (Ps. 119:11).

Theology Leads to Worship

I'll wrap up my last point, following Paul and other biblical writers, that in the end theology is ultimately about worship. Yes, it informs our thinking. Yes, it shapes our feelings. And yes, it instructs us on how to live rightly before God and others. But when we think about it, all of the benefits that doing theology brings converge on a single point: making much of Jesus.

This was often the case for the biblical writers in the New Testament. For instance, after having elaborated on the deepest and greatest theological truths imaginable for eleven chapters, Paul broke out into a hymn of praise, saying:

> Oh, the depth of the riches both of the wisdom and the knowledge of God! How unsearchable His judgments and untraceable His ways! For who has known the mind of the Lord? Or who has been His counselor? Or who has ever first given to Him, and has to be repaid? For from Him and through Him and to Him are all things. To Him be the glory forever. Amen. (Rom. 11:33-36)

For Paul and other writers of Scripture, praise and worship was the natural outcome of good theology. When we rightly understand who Jesus is with our minds and delight in the person and work of Christ with our hearts, the praise and worship of Christ will follow.

Of course, worship isn't merely what takes place on Sunday mornings or Wednesday night youth services. Worship is primarily from the heart, which then paves the way to a life of worship. It begins with a heart that hates and avoids sin, while loving and pursuing what is good. We see this clearly demonstrated when the psalmist declared, "I have treasured Your word in my heart so that I may not sin against You" (Ps. 119:11). Thus, when genuine worship of God takes root deep within us, that worship will eventually overflow into our daily lives and influence everything we do.

This point alone is enough to convince Christians that theology is a noble task worth pursuing. There are lots of benefits we can point to as to why doing theology would be helpful to grow and mature us as Christians, but in the end, theology helps us to be better worshipers of King Jesus.

QUESTIONS FOR DISCUSSION

1. What was your definition of theology before this study? How will you view theology now?

2. Why is a solid foundation in theology so vital in our ever-changing culture?

3. What are some practical steps you can take to deepen your knowledge of God? How does this help you have a right relationship with Him?

4. How can you guard against compartmentalizing your life as a Christian?

5. How does solid theology help you live out biblical manhood? What does this look like for you as a young man?

6. Where do you tend to look to find your identity? How can you commit to living in the truth that Christ is in you?

7. What role do faith and works play in our lives as believers in Christ?

8. How does it give you hope to know that God is sovereign and equips us to endure tough situations? How does this affect the way you live?

9. How does the information you've learned in this chapter lead you into deeper relationship with God?

10. In what ways does good theology affect our worship? How will this affect you personally?

CHAPTER 3

SPIRITUAL DISCIPLINES

ABOUT THE AUTHOR

Zachary Ethridge *is a student pastor at Liberty Baptist Church in Hampton, Virginia. He is a graduate of Liberty University, and recently earned his MTS from Southwestern Baptist Theological Seminary. Zac and his wife, Tori, are expecting their first child, Ella Grace, in August 2016.*

Spiritual disciplines are works that we do in order to cultivate our relationship with God and practice our faith in Him. You read that correctly—spiritual disciplines are works. These disciplines are the highways that enable us to seek the Lord, the means through which we experience and obey God. You may not realize it, but you were made to know your Creator, who has made Himself known in and through Jesus Christ. "He is the image of the invisible God" (Col. 1:15); "He is the radiance of God's glory and the exact expression of His nature" (Heb. 1:3). As we begin to talk about seeking Him, let's first remember that He has sought us. The fact that you're reading this sentence is evidence of God's pursuit of you. God loves us and initiates a relationship with us because the best gift He can give us is Himself.

No one enters into a personal relationship with their almighty Creator and responds with disinterest. You can know God personally through faith in Jesus Christ, and your faith will certainly produce seeking. You will want to know Him more. When your spiritual senses are awakened to experience the glory of Christ, make no mistake about it—your faith will produce the work of spiritual discipline. I'm not trying to suggest that it will be easy. Your sinful nature will fight you every day—you will be tempted to quit. When this happens, you must remember why God calls us to pursue the spiritual disciplines. If you do them for any other reason other than to deepen your relationship with God, you will quit. I have no doubt that you will give up, unless you remember that spiritual disciplines are the means through which we can know and experience the God who made us for a relationship with Himself (Isa. 43:7; 1 Peter 3:15).

This intense focus, this discipline, isn't called a discipline because it's easy. It's a battle, and the stakes couldn't be higher. "Rehoboam did what was evil, because he did not determine in his heart to seek the LORD" (2 Chron. 12:14). But the Psalmist said, "Young lions lack food and go hungry, but those who seek the LORD will not lack any good thing" (Ps. 34:10), and "he has satisfied the thirsty, and filled the hungry with good things" (Ps. 107:9). The bottom line is this: When you're seeking God, it will always be worth it. God calls us to this rewarding pursuit in the spiritual disciplines. So, what exactly are the spiritual disciplines?

BIBLE STUDY

The Bible is the primary means through which God has made Himself known to us. It is our primary source for learning who God is and how He has revealed Himself in Jesus Christ. Therefore studying God's Word is absolutely essential to spiritual growth. Remember, the goal of practicing spiritual disciplines is to know God more. Therefore, studying His Word, through which He has revealed Himself, is the foundation of all the other disciplines. The Word gives shape to the rest of our lives.

Moreover, God's Word is the primary way that we can know how to seek Him. When we speak of "seeking God," we're referring to specific practices that are prescribed in Scripture. We are not free to pursue God however we see fit. Rather, the spiritual disciplines are the avenues that lead believers closer to God. They are the specific means through which we are transformed by the Holy Spirit into the image of Christ. We wouldn't be able to know or understand how to carry out these specific means without the special revelation of the Bible. How could we know that prayer and fasting are ways to cultivate our relationship with God, apart from the Scriptures telling us? God alone can set the parameters of what it looks like to seek Him. Therefore, we must place Bible study at the top of the list when it comes to spiritual disciplines. It wouldn't be possible to know any other spiritual disciplines apart from studying God's Word.

Still, Bible study isn't just a way to learn about other disciplines—it is a discipline. In Scripture, God has revealed various life habits to help us grow in our relationship with Him. However, the Bible is not primarily the revelation of spiritual disciplines. First and foremost, the Bible is the revelation of God. Therefore, studying Scripture with any other aim other than to know God through Christ is a waste of time.

In God's Word, we find that He is omnipotent (all powerful), and omniscient (all knowing). He is inexhaustibly gracious and His love is unending. He is truthful, righteous, and just in all He does. We are only able to know these things about God because of the Bible. You will only accurately perceive God when you have a clearer view of His character as revealed in His Word. This brings me to another important concept. When I talk about knowing God, I don't just mean knowing about God; I mean knowing Him personally. However, it's critical to understand that you do have to know *about* God in order to know Him.

You have probably heard people say, "It's not enough to know about God, you have to know Him personally." Though there's an element of truth to this statement, it's incomplete. Who is your closest friend? I'm sure you know a lot more about him than I ever will. My closest friend is my wife, and one of the reasons that we are so close is because we know so much about each other. In the Scriptures, God is saying to us, "I want you to know Me; therefore, here is everything your finite mind can handle about Me." So, yes and amen to all the talk about having more than just a head knowledge of God, but since you're already hearing this from everyone else, let me stand on the other end of the scale for a moment and say: "Don't expect to know God when you're content to know so little about Him." Study the Bible!

As you begin to study the Bible more, be careful not to lose sight of the fact that God makes Himself known through Christ. It is entirely possible to believe the Bible is inspired by God, read it regularly, and still be far from God. Jesus told the Jews that their commitment to the Bible was useless, because they failed to see that the Scriptures "testify about [Him]" (John 5:39). Again in John 5:46, Jesus said, "For if you believed Moses, you would believe Me, because he wrote about Me." It is for this reason that studying the Bible is a spiritual discipline—it is a way to know Christ, a way to have a growing relationship with God.

In the greatest sermon ever preached, Jesus said, "Don't assume that I came to destroy the Law or the Prophets. I did not come to destroy but to fulfill" (Matt. 5:17). The phrase "the Law and the Prophets" was a reference to the Old Testament—Jesus was claiming that the story of the Bible is ultimately about Him. If you're serious about knowing Jesus, you will be serious about studying the Bible—it's ultimately about Jesus. That is not to say that the Bible is only about Jesus, but it is finally and ultimately about Him. If this is a foreign idea to you, consider the fact that Jesus started with the Old Testament and worked His way through the Scriptures to reveal Himself to His disciples (Luke 24:27). This isn't to say that every passage of Scripture is about Jesus explicitly, but that every time we read the Bible, we should do so with the work of Christ in mind.

Daily Bible reading apart from a commitment to the hard work of faithfully interpreting the Scripture is more dangerous than driving with no regard for the road signs and traffic lights. Here are two guiding principles to use as you study:

1. **Seek to understand the historical context and what God intended to reveal to the text's original audience.**

   We need to remember that the Bible isn't ultimately about us. It is about Jesus. It is only when we first understand this that we will be prepared to apply it our context in life-giving ways. Furthermore, we need to recognize that the Bible was originally written to specific people in specific contexts. The passages are true historical accounts, and God intended the original readers to learn and apply that knowledge to their lives. Here are some questions to ask in order to help us read in context.

   » Who are the main characters? What is their situation?
   » How did the author expect the original audience to respond to the passage?
   » How may God expect us to apply this passage? Are there ways we should imitate the characters or learn from their mistakes?

Like Jesus said, these texts point to something beyond themselves. They are part of a bigger narrative. This leads us to our second principle.

2. **Seek to understand how the cultural historical context fits into God's story of redemption.**

   Sometimes we get tunnel vision while reading stories in the Bible. These are not isolated stories, unnaturally forced together to create the Bible. Rather, God supernaturally orchestrated and authored each story with one grand story in mind—a story that puts His glory on full display in the person and work of Jesus Christ. Keep these questions in mind to help you see the relation of each story to the overall work of Jesus Christ.

» Does it directly point to Jesus? If not, how does this story relate to Jesus?

» How does this text illuminate or reveal elements of the gospel (*God's holiness, sin, faith, atonement, etc.*)?

» Are there people in His story who give us glimpses of Christ's work for His people? If, so how?

Again, every single verse by itself is not about Jesus and the gospel; the authors weren't even thinking in terms of verses. They were writing history, poetry, and letters to churches. Some verses directly prophesy about Jesus, others narrow the possibilities of the Messiah's identity. Still others show us elements of the gospel—like the justice of God, the sinfulness of man, the need for atonement, and the necessity of faith. Some people in the Old Testament function as *symbols* or *forerunners* of the Messiah, revealing something of what Jesus would be like and what He would accomplish. Although all of the biblical stories don't talk about Jesus in the exact same way, God uses the entire Bible to reveal Himself through His Son, Jesus. No study of the Bible is sufficient until it takes into account the words of Jesus in Luke 24, and responds by acknowledging that the entirety of the Bible is about Him.

COMMUNITY AND ACCOUNTABILITY

Studying the Bible is something that should become very personal to you, but it must not remain only personal. Following Christ requires studying His Word intimately and in community (2 Tim. 3:16-17; Eph. 4:15). If we hope to grow in Christ, we must study the Bible with other believers who will challenge us to mature and grow. As you seek God personally, it's critical that you allow other Christians to speak into your personal experience with God. It could be some friends from church, a brother, your parents, or your youth pastor. We call this *accountability*, which is helpful and necessary for a number of reasons. First, it creates space for honesty and vulnerability. As we struggle to understand a text or fight to obey a command, we need to know God has not left us alone. When you share about your time in God's Word with other believers, you will be strengthened and encouraged. They will help you guard against misunderstandings and misinterpretations. They will support you as you attempt to obey a particular passage. Moreover, as you verbalize what God is teaching you, it will often deepen your understanding and affection for God and bring you into a greater enjoyment of His Word.

No one naturally delights in spiritual truth. Your flesh is hostile to God and does not want to read and submit to His Word (Rom. 8:7). Ultimately, we need the Holy Spirit to open our eyes to see the greatness of Christ and the beauty of the gospel (1 Cor. 2:10-16). However, when we give other guys the green light to hold us to our commitment to personally study the Bible, God uses their encouragement and our efforts to create a habit. Although you may not love to read God's Word today, as you study it on a daily basis your desire will grow. My brother-in-law is from Canada, and before moving to the United States, sweet tea was not a regular part of his diet. As he spent more time with our family, he was encouraged to try it. He didn't immediately want it at every meal, but over time he acquired a taste for sweet tea. Studying God's Word is similar. Naturally, we don't enjoy the meal of biblical truth. It tastes foreign to our souls. But by God's grace, as we make it a fundamental part of our daily routine, the Spirit alters the taste buds of our souls.

As we read the Scriptures each day, we learn to crave the Bread of life (John 6:35) and living Water (John 7:37-39). We will find that "in [God's] presence is abundant joy; in [His] right hand are eternal pleasures" (Ps. 16:11). As we behold the glory of the Lord, we will be transformed (2 Cor. 3:18). We will be changed because a craving for the Scriptures will lead to a hunger and thirst for righteousness. The Bible functions like a window, through which we perceive the life-giving beauty of God and the ugliness of sin.

When I look back on the different seasons of my spiritual journey, I see a pattern. I am always closest to God when I read God's Word on a daily basis and allow other believers to speak into my relationship with Him. I am convinced that there is a causal relationship between our daily study of Scripture and our personal experience of God. I emphasize this discipline because understanding and knowing God as He reveals Himself should give shape and color to every other spiritual discipline.

Take a moment to consider the excuses you make for why you don't read your Bible on a daily basis. Maybe your excuse is something like "I just don't have time." I remember one time I told my mom that I didn't have time to bring my laundry downstairs every day. She wittingly responded by saying, "You always have enough time to do what you really want to do." She was right. It didn't matter how full my day was, if I wanted to play a video game, I made the time to play. If I wanted to call my girlfriend, I made time to talk. If there was a football game I wanted to watch, I ensured that I could be in front of the TV in time for the kickoff. Think about how many hours a week you spend on social media, playing sports, watching TV, or playing video games. You definitely have time to study the Bible.

I used to get up at 5:30 a.m. every Tuesday and Thursday to play basketball. In that same season of life, I struggled to wake up early to read my Bible. Why would I jump out of bed before the sun had risen to play a game, but neglect to do the same every morning to spend time with God? First, I had accountability to play basketball that I didn't have with my Bible study. If I didn't go, I knew I'd be getting texts and phone calls challenging me to be there next time. But more than that, I acquired a desire to play, even though I wasn't thrilled about the start time at the beginning. Again, you and I definitely have time to study the Bible. The question is whether we really want to and if we've structured the relationships in our lives in such a way that holds us to our commitment even when we don't feel like it. By God's grace, you will come to a point in your life when you won't be able to imagine a day apart from seeking God in His Word.

When your alarm goes off in the morning, remember that the main reason you're alive is to glorify your Maker. How will you know how to do that apart from His instruction? How will you display His image in the world if you don't know what He's like? God gets glory as He is on display because He is the most glorious Being in the universe. So, open your Bible where He can be found. Find Him to be the treasure and promise keeper that He is. More than anything, seek to know and see His Son so you can be made like Him.

PRAYER

While studying the Bible is the primary spiritual discipline, it doesn't stand alone at the top. In fact, as we are reading the Bible, prayer is often what God uses to illuminate the truth of the passage in our hearts and minds. I know it's not the most revolutionary thing you've ever heard, but in this culture of trendiness, men of God need to go back to the basics. There are no shortcuts to getting closer to God, He has made the path clear. You have to read His Word and pray. Anyone who plans on being close to God needs to plan on cultivating a lifestyle of prayer, including specific times that you set aside to pray and spontaneous prayer throughout your daily activities.

Maybe you're reading this thinking you will never be able to form a habit of prayer. If you find it difficult to pray, don't be discouraged—even the disciples were confused about how to pray. The disciples even asked Jesus to teach them how to pray, to which Jesus responded by teaching them what we call "The Lord's Prayer" (Luke 11:1-4). That prayer is also found in Matthew 6, where Jesus gives some important instructions before giving the example prayer. Nothing I say about prayer would be more helpful for you than Jesus' own words. Matthew 6:5-13 reads:

> "Whenever you pray, you must not be like the hypocrites, because they love to pray standing in the synagogues and on the street corners to be seen by people. I assure you: They've got their reward! But when you pray, go into your private room, shut your door, and pray to your Father who is in secret. And your Father who sees in secret will reward you. When you pray, don't babble like the idolaters, since they imagine they'll be heard for their many words. Don't be like them, because your Father knows the things you need before you ask Him. "Therefore, you should pray like this: Our Father in heaven, Your name be honored as holy. Your kingdom come. Your will be done on earth as it is in heaven. Give us today our daily bread. And forgive

us our debts, as we also have forgiven our debtors.
And do not bring us into temptation, but deliver us
from the evil one. [For Yours is the kingdom and
the power and the glory forever. Amen.]"

There is nothing wrong with praying when others are around. In fact, the Book of Acts gives us countless examples of how we should pray together. Jesus' point is that prayer shouldn't be a performance. Rather, prayer is a genuine conversation with God. You don't have to use fancy, big, or complicated words. Maybe you're embarrassed to talk to God because you think you won't sound smart enough, but guess what—God is not impressed by our words (Matt. 6: 5-8; 1 Cor. 2:1).

When my younger nieces and nephews want to talk to me, I don't look down on their mispronunciations and poor phrasing. I'm thrilled that they are learning and growing! Likewise, I have a brother-in-law from Argentina. When he was first learning English, I was just happy that he was trying to have a conversation with me. I'm sure when I tried to speak Spanish, he was thankful that I attempted to communicate with him and build our relationship. It is similar with God. He knows our hearts, and He doesn't need our fancy religious talk. In fact, He isn't impressed by it (Matt. 6:7). For example, the prayers of the psalmists are often honest and desperate rather than careful and calculated: they cry out to God, "How long, O LORD?" (Ps. 13, ESV). He just wants you to seek Him. His ear is open because the Jesus' sacrifice on the cross has reconciled us to Him, not because we have a big theological vocabulary. Pray with confidence.

If you're anything like me, Matthew 6:8 raises a question—if God already knows what I need before I pray, why do I need to pray at all? The truth of the matter is that God does already know everything. Our prayers don't inform Him of anything new. However, prayer is still a vital part of your spiritual life, because it is an expression of faith in God. When you take a request to God, your actions reveal that you believe He is in control of the universe. Also, the act of praying perfects your faith. Prayer is a humbling act—it reminds us that we are needy and opens our eyes to the strength of the One who can truly help us. Furthermore, prayer helps us to align our will with God's. This is by no means an exhaustive list of reasons to pray, but I hope it helps you see why it's crucial to bring your requests to God even though He knows the details before you ask.

Let's consider the content of The Lord's Prayer. Jesus said, "Our Father in heaven" (Matt. 6:9). Prayer is personal—God is our Father, not a cosmic stranger. And He is in heaven ruling and reigning, working and watching. As I said before, prayer acknowledges that God is in control. The next line says, "Your name be honored as holy" (v. 9). Worship is at the very heart of prayer. We come to Him with praise, and all of our prayers ought to have His exaltation as the final aim. Then Jesus said, "Your kingdom come. Your will be done on earth as it is in heaven" (v. 10). Again, when we pray, we align our plans with God's plans. This is a way of expressing how God's ways are better than ours, and that we want His perfect will to be shown through our daily activities. Then, Jesus concluded His prayer with an expression of dependence. In prayer, we come face to face with the reality that we aren't autonomous, meaning we are not self-sufficient. He is the source of all life, and we desperately need Him to sustain us both physically and spiritually. Therefore, we pray for the things we need. We confess sins, seek forgiveness, and lean on Him for victory over sin. In summary, Jesus shows us in these verses that biblical prayer is undeniably God-centered. Biblical prayer it's about His glory, His will, and His provision.

There is another essential element of prayer in Matthew 6:9-13. Notice that the personal pronouns Jesus used were not singular. Jesus used "our" (v. 9) and "us" (v. 11). I think two things are in play here. First, He assumed that we would pray together, in community. However, that cannot be the only explanation, because this passage also includes His instruction for us to pray privately (vv. 5-6). God expects us to not only pray with one another, but to also pray for one another (Jas. 5:16). Few things align your heart with God's like praying for your family, other believers, and the world. It will absolutely change the way that you live. I find it more difficult to fight with my wife when I have been lifting her up in prayer. It's hard to be bitter toward people at church when you have been interceding for them throughout the week. You will have an evangelist's heart toward the world when you regularly pray for your neighbors and the nations. One day soon, you will become one of the men God uses to lead families, churches, and the world. They need you, but more than anything, they need God. You will lead and serve them best when you continually go before God on their behalf.

Today it seems like few men are dedicated to prayer. Why is that? Every day we are engaged in spiritual warfare (Eph. 6:10-19), and yet men seem to be the last one's are willing to fight on the front lines. Maybe it's because we don't feel manly when we express dependence upon God. Whatever the reason, allowing your pride to keep you from interceding for others causes you to abandon the people God is calling you to love, lead, and protect, leaving them out on the battlefield with no cover. We need a generation of young men who will go to war in prayer for their families, friends, and the world.

When I think about the men who have come before us— Moses, David, Elijah—they were men of prayer. Imagine the hours that Moses spent interceding for the Israelites before the Lord. Think of all the prayers that David recorded in the Book of Psalms. Where are the men, like Elijah, who are calling down the fire of God on this world? Take a minute and think about the commitment to prayer that we see in the apostles throughout the New Testament. Men of God are prayer warriors. When was the last time you begged God to have mercy on others like Abraham did for Sodom? God wants "the men in every place to pray" (1 Tim. 2:8). You and I are no exception. So let's stop with all the excuses, and cry out to Him who has the power to accomplish His good purposes in the world.

To this point, we have covered the most fundamental spiritual disciplines. However, there are other life habits that you will need to develop in order to cultivate your relationship with God and practice your faith in Him.

WORSHIP

This word *worship* is common, yet rarely clearly defined. So, here's my attempt at articulating a definition for us. Worship is an inward awe for God that is a response to His immeasurable worth, which often results in an external expression of praise. This definition certainly includes singing, but it doesn't exclusively refer to singing. Rather, worship is a way of life. It characterizes the life of a person who has encountered the glory of God through the person and work of Christ.

With that said, I do want to take a moment to consider the need for regular corporate and personal worship in the narrow sense we usually use the word. The overwhelming pattern in Scripture is that the people of God gathered to collectively stand in awe of God and express their wonder with singing. As we sing and study Scripture, our focus shifts from ourselves to Christ.

Our mind's attention and our heart's affections are fixed upon our Creator. As we actively participate in corporate worship with the intent to see and submit to Christ, our relationship with Him is strengthened.

However, that won't be enough. If you're anything like me, your flesh doesn't just fight against your soul on Sundays and Wednesdays. That's why we need daily Scripture reading, prayer, and worship. Every day, your human nature and desires will try to drown out your godly living. Your only hope is to delight in God. So, here's my question—what are you doing each day to stir your affection for God? Are you seeking Him in His Word, seeking Him in prayer, and singing praise to Him? If you're listening to Christian music, great! But let me challenge you further, because not all "Christian" music helps us engage in worship—much of it was written to be clean, Christian entertainment, not a response to God's glory. So, intentionally search for music that was written specifically for worship. We aren't aiming for clean entertainment; we're aiming for inward awe that results in praise.

MEDITATION AND JOURNALING

Meditation and journaling are two ways to make your study, prayer, and worship more fruitful. While other religions such as Buddhism and Hinduism encourage meditation in the sense of emptying ourselves of all thought, Christianity encourages a type of mediation in which we fill ourselves with truth. Christian meditation is the simple practice of thinking deeply on the truth of God's Word for the purpose of delighting in God and growing in obedience to Him (Ps. 119:9-16). Journaling means recording your insights from God's Word, answers to prayer, and your progress in your walk with Christ.

We are the most over-stimulated generation in the history of mankind, yet we have lost the art of feeling the weightiness of spiritual truth. Great sermons and worship songs are written by those who pause to deeply consider the things of God. Meditation and journaling are the disciplines that create the necessary time and space for spiritual truths soak into your soul. When you read, think about what the Scripture means, wrestle with it in your mind. When you sing, consciously reflect on lyrics. As details of a biblical passage stand out to you, jot them down. When your heart is full of pain or joy, take a moment to spell out your thoughts. This kind of meditation and journaling will result in meaningful growth.

STEWARDSHIP

Stewardship is all about using our resources in a way that demonstrates an understanding of the fact that everything belongs to God. We own nothing—not ourselves or our belongings—everything is on loan from God. Everything in heaven and on earth belongs to God (1 Chron. 29:11). When a man invents a new product, he has all the rights to what made. Likewise, when a man buys a car, he has authority over how it's used. We have been created and purchased by God. When we use our lives to display that ownership, it is called stewardship. Stewardship is about more than money. It's about our hearts and minds, time, things, and money. As a man who will one day be charged with the task of providing for his family, I can assure you it will not always be easy to give. Giving financially to the Kingdom is an expression of faith in God's provision. It's a way of reminding yourself and expressing to others that everything belongs to God.

avenues to know and glorify God, then yes. But if you see these practices as ways to experience and enjoy Him, then absolutely not! It's not legalistic to demand that we practice our faith in the way God's Word calls us to. Rather, legalism is turning the disciplines into gods themselves. By all means, use the effort and strength that God supplies to cultivate and carry out your faith. Remember the words of the apostle Paul, "I worked more than any of them, yet not I, but God's grace that was with me" (1 Cor. 15:10). My prayer for you is that God would "by His power, fulfill every desire for goodness and the work of faith" (2 Thess. 1:11). Even when it seems like you aren't making any progress, keep seeking God and eventually you will see the resulting closeness in your relationship with Him (Gal. 6:9). Remember the instruction in God's Word and put it into practice, continually (1 Thess. 4:1). Whether you've been practicing these disciplines for five days or five years, continue to do so more and more. No matter how much we mature as believers in this life, we haven't arrived.

Finally, as you begin to practice these spiritual disciplines, keep in mind Philippians 2:12b–13 which says, "Work out your own salvation with fear and trembling. For it is God who is working in you, enabling you both to desire and to work out His good purpose." Did you catch that? You "work out" your salvation as God works in you! Spiritual growth is like surfing. No one surfs on a pond; it's impossible! The surfer is totally dependent upon a force outside of himself to move him forward. However, you will never find a great surfer who isn't working with all of his might. He is paddling hard, getting in the right position, and doing his best to balance. He is depending upon the wave 100 percent, and he is giving 100 percent effort. That's how spiritual growth happens. If want to move forward, it'll be because an outside force (God) is providing all the power to get to the destination.

Like the wave, He will also be there, time and time again. The question is whether you will simply lie on your surf board, or start paddling as hard as you can. Are you seeking the Lord? Are you practicing the spiritual disciplines? I promise it will be worth it. I pray that in the end, your testimony will be like that of the Psalmist who wrote, "Yet I am always with You; You hold my right hand. You guide me with Your counsel, and afterward You will take me up in glory" (Ps. 73:23–24).

QUESTIONS FOR DISCUSSION

1. Why do you think reading Scripture and praying are considered the most vital spiritual disciplines?

2. Do you have people who hold you accountable to studying God's Word? If so, thank God for those people. If not, commit to finding someone this week.

3. Why do you think community and accountability are so important to your walk with God?

4. Discuss the two practical tips given for studying God's Word. How can you work to understand the historical context for the biblical audience, as well as how it fits into God's overall story of redemption?

5. According to the model of the Lord's prayer, what should be the purpose of our prayers?

6. In what ways is worship more thank what we do in church? Why is this important to realize? Why is corporate worship still important as well?

7. How is meditation often misunderstood? Why is this an important practice of the Christian faith?

8. Why is it important to realize everything on earth belongs to God and we are His stewards? What steps will you take this week to be a better steward of the things God has given you?

9. What is the purpose of fasting? How can we guard against simplifying this to no more than restraint from eating?

10. How can you engage in evangelism where you are now?

CHAPTER 4

PERSONAL HOLINESS

ABOUT THE AUTHOR

Clayton King *is an evangelist, founder and president of Crossroads Summer Camps, and a Teaching Pastor at Newspring Church. He and his wife, Sharie, re-wrote* True Love Waits *for a new generation, entitled* True Love Project, *which recently won the Young Adult Book of the Year award from the Christian Retailers Association. He is the author of 13 books and hosts his own TV show, "Stronger with Clayton King." He is also Distinguished Professor of Evangelism at Anderson University. You can hear more from Clayton at* www.claytonking.com.

Look around and you will see people chasing all sorts of dreams. Popularity. Success. Financial security. Living debt free. A college scholarship. The honor roll. A strong, muscular body. A bigger house. Getting elected. Becoming valedictorian or team captain. So what are you chasing? What's your primary pursuit? Have you ever asked yourself what you're really living for? Have you ever even thought about it? What is your "big win" in life?

I want you to think about it. I want you to settle it, right here and right now if you haven't already made your decision. But before you do, I want to speak with you openly. Allow me to help you consider what it actually is that you want to gain, specifically in your relationship with God.

What if I told you that God clearly spells out what He expects from us, taking away the mystery and confusion of what God really wants? And what if I could show you two places in the Bible where He specifically instructs us on what we should pursue?

Jesus helps us answer the question of what the big win in life should be. In John 17:3 He said, "This is eternal life: that they may know You, the only true God, and the One You have sent—Jesus Christ." In essence, knowing God through a relationship with Jesus is the ultimate win. That should be your primary goal, the bedrock that you build your life upon. Regardless of failures and successes, wins and losses, accolades and accomplishments, that and that alone should be our ultimate pursuit.

So how do we get there? First, we have to understand that God sent Jesus to the earth on a mission of redeeming and restoring everything lost in the fall. He came to seek and save the lost and to forgive sin. He died the death we deserved on the cross and rose from the dead to give us new life. When the Father sent Jesus here, He set Him apart. The word for this is holy, which means set apart and chosen for a purpose. Holiness is intentionally and deliberately being different because you've been set apart on purpose, for a purpose. Now, let's look at something Peter said. This was the same Peter who spent three and half years following Jesus, denied Him, and was eventually reinstated as the leader of the New Testament church:

> Therefore, with your minds ready for action, be serious and set your hope completely on the grace to be brought to you at the revelation of Jesus Christ. As obedient children, do not be conformed to the desires of your former ignorance. *But as the One who called you is holy, you also are to be holy in all your conduct; for it is written, Be holy, because I am holy.* (1 Pet. 1:13-16, emphasis mine)

And there it is, straight from the Bible, from the mouth of Jesus and the hand of Peter. Growing in holiness should be our goal as we pursue the ultimate big win in life—knowing Jesus. So if having a relationship is the destination, then holiness is the direction you take in getting there. We must be holy because God is holy, and we belong to God. He makes us holy. Then He expects us to live like holy people, set apart for the purpose of knowing Jesus and making His gospel known. We do this by proclaiming to the world around us God's glory and love for humanity.

DIRECTION AND DESTINATION

How happy is everyone who fears the Lᴏʀᴅ, who walks in His ways! (Ps. 128:1)

"Everyone ends up somewhere, but few people end up somewhere on purpose."[1] —Craig Groeschel

Soon after I graduated from college, some friends of mine from another state decided they were going to come visit my roommates and me while they were on a road trip. As young, single guys our house was always open to buddies that needed a place to crash for the night or just drop in. We were excited to have guests. We were going to eat pizza, watch sports, and stay up really late. I specifically told them how to get to our house. Since I traveled for a living as an evangelist and speaker, I was meticulous about directions. My livelihood depended on having clear directions to my destination.

I told them, "When you get near Spartanburg on I-26, begin looking for signs for I-85. Take I-85 North until you see signs for Highway 150. Take that exit into Boiling Springs." They said they would be at our house about 3 p.m.

We kept waiting, but they never showed up. Several hours after they said they would arrive, they called me from a gas station just north of Atlanta. "Clayton, you live in North Carolina, right? For some reason we are in Georgia. We did exactly what you said. We drove up from Columbia, South Carolina to Spartanburg and then we got on I-85."

It took me less than second to realize what they had done. They were on the right interstate, but in the wrong state. They were on the right road, but going the wrong direction. I told them to go north. They went south. It was the right road, but the wrong direction, and the wrong direction always leads to the wrong destination.

They really wanted to come to my house, but they were heading the wrong way, and no matter how far they drove, how frustrated they became, or how many people they asked for help, the only way they were ever going to arrive at their desired destination was to change directions. They needed to turn around.

In the same way, we don't gain holiness by trying harder. We become holy by turning around. The word for this turnaround is repent, which means to do an about-face, to be walking one way and decide to turn completely around and go in the opposite direction. Holiness begins when you realize you're living your life selfishly, controlled by appetites and desires that lead to sin. Then, the Holy Spirit convicts you that there is a better way to live by giving your life to Jesus. You confess your sins to God. You own up to your mistakes and ask God to take over your life. You trust in Jesus and His sacrifice on the cross for you. You ask Him to save you. You surrender your life to Him.

This is what it means to turn around. You're heading in a new direction now. And for the first time in your life, a Holy God dwells within you. His presence inside of you makes you holy—new, set apart, and different. When you do this, you're heading in the right direction and it will get you to the right destination.

Andy Stanley says it's direction, not intention that leads to a destination.[2] This seems like common sense, but so few people seem to follow this wisdom. Yet if you want to enjoy a relationship with God and fellowship with your sisters and brothers in Christ, you will need to apply this wisdom. And you need to begin now. You may need to turn around and change directions. You may need to decide where it is you want to wind up, because you're going to end up somewhere eventually. Why not go there intentionally?

Intentionality, however, is not enough. *It's not your intention that gets you to your destination. It's taking action by heading in the right direction.* Holiness is a gift given to you by Christ. Yet it is also a decision you make and a direction you choose; to live your life set apart by God for the purpose of bringing Him glory and living as a witness of the power of the gospel. If your intention is to honor the Lord with your life, your purity, and your thoughts and actions, then you will have to back that intention up with action. The journey toward holiness begins when you head in the right direction.

DESTINATION AND DISCIPLINE

Holiness is both a destination and a discipline. If we want to live a holy life, if we desire to be holy because our God is holy, we must be disciplined. Think of holiness in the context of the phrase *now and not yet*. We are holy now because Jesus gave us His holiness when we received Him by faith as Lord and Savior. However, we are not yet completely holy because we still struggle against sin and temptation. Living in the grace God gives us to be holy requires faith and effort on our part each day. So, if you belong to Jesus, you are holy now, but you are not yet as holy as you will be when Christ returns and we are made new in heaven.

Before you can strike out in the right direction, you must decide where it is you want to go, and I'm not only talking about going to heaven when you die. I'm talking about deciding what kind of man you want to be. Without that crucial piece of information settled at the outset, you're wasting time and energy going nowhere. Think about what the psalmist was saying when he wrote these words:

> Your word is a lamp for my feet and a light on my
> path. I have taken an oath and confirmed it, that I will
> follow your righteous laws. (Ps. 119:105-106, NIV)

He seems to think of his life as a journey, like a man walking along a path. But that path is dark and he cannot see where he is going or what may lie along the path to trip him. He is on the right road, but to make sure he is heading in the right direction, he has chosen to light the way with God's Word. He solemnly swears to live by Scripture, to submit himself to God and His ways, and to allow God's wisdom to illuminate the dark and expose any trap or temptation that could hurt him. He believes God's Word is his only hope for arriving at his destination. He makes the effort to take an oath and then commits himself to keeping that oath for the sake of living a holy life for God's glory.

The method he uses to stay focused on the right direction is simple—he remembers God's instructions. He remembers God's precepts. He remembers God's decrees. He celebrates them! They give him joy!

> My life is constantly in danger, yet I do not forget
> your instruction. The wicked have set a trap for
> me, but I have not wandered from your precepts.
> I have your decrees as a heritage forever; indeed,
> they are the joy of my heart. I am resolved to obey
> your statutes to the very end. (Ps. 119:109-112)

He made a serious commitment to obey God saying, "I am resolved to obey your statutes until I reach my destination." He knows where he wants to go, and he knows the only way to get there is to fix his eyes and his heart on God and His Word. Do you want to be holy, set apart for God's purpose for your life? If you do, then here's how:

> How can a young man stay on the path of purity?
> By living according to your word. I seek you
> with all my heart; do not let me stray from your
> commands. I have hidden your word in my heart
> that I might not sin against you. (Ps. 119:9-11, NIV)

Holiness is just a word until you act on your desire for Christ. We must submit ourselves to the Bible, because the more we read, know, love, memorize, and meditate on it, the more we will see how worthless sin is compared to the beauty of Jesus. This is the direction we take toward a life of holiness. We walk the path that is illuminated by God's Word. This journey won't be easy. We will trip and fall. And when we do, God will forgive us and help us repent.

TAKE ACTION

It's not enough to have good intentions when it comes to holiness, a Godly marriage, or resisting temptations like porn, lust, and sex. You have to take action. So how do you actively pursue holiness? Where do you start? Allow me illustrate the necessity of taking action immediately in the area of personal holiness.

I'm a football kind of guy. I played for 14 years. I love college football and the NFL. I watch as many games as possible. Even though this happened to me 25 years ago, it's still as fresh in my mind as if it happened this morning. I tried out for varsity football as a freshman. I was told that I had virtually no shot at making the team at such a young age, but I decided to go for it and it paid off. I made the team and even started the first game of the season.

Among the many things our head coach taught us was the danger of "standing around on the field." During a play, you had to keep moving. If you stopped, it was guaranteed that a player on the other team would see you standing still and interpret that as an invitation to knock your head off. If you weren't moving, you were a target. My coach yelled and screamed constantly about this. He warned us that we could get seriously hurt if we didn't keep moving down the field.

In my very first game as a varsity football player, I experienced what my coach had warned me about. I snapped the ball to the quarterback, blocked the nose guard, and watched our running back get tackled a few yards down the field. As I stood still watching him go down, a guy from the other team came at me like a bullet from a gun barrel. All I saw was a white streak to my left a split second before he hit me with the force of a comet. He knocked me out cold, all because I stopped moving.

My coach didn't have a crystal ball. He just had common sense and experience. I should have listened to him, but I had to learn the hard way. If you just stand around doing nothing, you will get blindsided. You will give in to temptation. Whether a cute girl, a keg party, or cheating on exam at school, you have to stay aggressive in fighting temptation Holiness is not a spectator sport; it requires movement and action.

THE FIRST STEP

We all know intuitively that we can't do this without help. God knows this better than we do, so He has given us His Word to guide and instruct us in our pursuit of holiness. I like to think of it like this:

Submission → Direction → Instruction → Action → Destination

Submission

Give up your rights as your own lord and surrender total control of your thoughts and relationships to God. Trust God fully with your future. Believe that He loves you and would never tell you to do something that was bad for you. Remember, He doesn't want anything from you. He wants something for you. You are too small to be lord of your own life. Let God call the shots, because He knows what's best for you. When you submit completely to Him, He sets you apart to show the world what He can do with a human life that's surrendered to Him. This is holiness on display.

Direction

Decide where you want to go and what kind of man you want to be. Look down the road of your life and imagine a marriage that is built on a solid foundation—not fickle feelings, but firm faith in Jesus. Imagine what kind of children you want to raise and the difference you want to make in the world. Dedicate yourself to moving toward that goal. Jot your ideas down in the margin of your Bible or your personal journal. Share your goal with your pastor, your parents, or your church. Pray that if you choose to remain single, you will find joy and fulfillment in Jesus and the church, being uniquely positioned to focus more energy on ministry and Kingdom work.

Instruction

Yield your mind and your heart to the wisdom of Scripture by reading, meditating on, and memorizing it. Ask an older, mature

Christian to mentor you. Submit to the authority of your pastor, your parents, and your spiritual leaders. Sit on the front row at church with a pen and a journal and take notes until your hand cramps up. Fill your iPhone with sermons to challenge you. Read books to instruct you in the ways of being a true disciple. Choose the voices you will listen to you and ignore the ones that don't encourage you to become more like Christ.

Action

Begin practicing the wisdom of God by actually doing what the Bible says on a regular basis, making application and obedience holy habits. Set standards for the people you will date. Put a filter on your computer. Ask some friends to check up on you and hold you accountable. Meet weekly with a pastor or a mentor. End a bad relationship that's pulling you down. Cancel your high speed Internet if you have to. Get off social media for a season. Avoid parties and social events where you will be tempted to hook up with girls. Get serious about Jesus and your destiny!

Destination

Believe this: Following Jesus by faith and living under His lordship will ultimately bring you joy and peace. Believe that if you desire to marry, that He will direct you to a godly woman you can share your life with when the time is right. If you can trust Jesus to save you from hell, you can trust His wisdom and will when it comes to love and relationships.

I hope you don't think I'm trying to give you a cute little formula to follow, because it's way more complex and involved than "five easy steps to holiness." With that said, the truth remains: There is a pattern and a rhythm to following Jesus as His disciple. The

Bible is filled with promises that God will fulfill His purpose in us if we remain faithful to Him through obedience. That's not a quick fix. It's an eternal promise from the living God!

PERFORMANCE, PERFECTION, AND POSITION

Guys are wired to fight for position. We internally want other people to notice us in the same way that we notice others. I naturally notice successful people and winning teams. My attention is drawn to loud noises, shiny cars, and big trucks—pretty much anything that stands out in its position. Anything prominent, guys tend to notice. If something or someone performs well—a team, a car, an athlete—then we pay attention. This can be a great personal motivation for us to do better in certain areas, like academics and athletics, but is not the best approach to personal holiness in our relationship with Jesus.

We can never perform perfectly in the Christian life (1 John 1:8-10). The good news is that God doesn't expect us to. He doesn't demand perfect behavior from you. Perfection is unattainable unless your name is Jesus Christ and you have nail scars in your hands and feet.

As a Christian, you have to decide how you will fight for your personal holiness. There are essentially two options—you can fight for holiness *with your performance*. Or you can fight for holiness *from your position*. Let me explain.

We are drawn to things that perform well. When a college football team begins slaughtering their opponents and wins a national championship, lots of new fans come out of the woodwork, wearing the jerseys and the hats of the team that has the momentum. The better the team performs, the more fans they gain. The better their performance, the higher their prominence.

We often apply the same thinking to our own fight for holiness. We tell ourselves that if we could just try harder and perform better, we would gain more victory in the areas where we struggle. *Stop lusting after that girl! Quit looking at porn! Stop thinking those sexual thoughts! Quit putting your hands where they don't belong!* Typically, the harder we try to be perfect, the more discouraged we become when we fail or mess up.

A better approach is to fight for holiness from your position. Instead of attempting to become pure by trying harder, you acknowledge that you are already pure in Christ because of His sacrifice on the cross for you. Your position is already secure. You are pure, holy, forgiven, and redeemed by His grace. You are not fighting *for* a position of holiness. You are fighting *from* a position of holiness.

Jesus doesn't give us prominence based on our performance. Instead, He gives us a new position based on His perfection. We must realize that in Christ and because of Jesus death and resurrection on your behalf, you are made holy. Being made holy means you are cleansed of sin and set apart. When we realize this we will have the kind of strength we need to walk in holiness.

This simple truth can liberate you from the pressure of always trying to be perfect. You know being perfect isn't possible, so see yourself from a new position. Jesus was perfect for you and He offers you His perfection as a gift. This actually leads to greater purity overall.

I was adopted when I was just a few weeks old. My birth mother was 15 when she gave birth to me, and she gave me to a family who could love and care for me. I always knew I was adopted, and my parents were clear that when I joined their family, I had all the rights and privileges as a member of that family. I gained a position in that family not based on my own actions, but based on their decision. *My position was secured by their decision.*

Your position as a child of God was secured by His decision to die in your place and give you His salvation. Now, all your actions flow from that position of perfection. You are perfect in Christ because you are already pure, forgiven, and clean.

FREEDOM IN SUBMISSION

Submit yourselves, then, to God. Resist the devil,
and he will flee from you. (Jas. 4:7, NIV)

Our strength is not based in human effort. Our strength to fight temptation comes from our willingness to submit to God, humbly relying on Him for strength. We deal with temptation differently when we submit to the lordship of Christ and His power to help us pursue holiness. The real battle is fought when we remember how powerless we are against an enemy as strong and seductive as sin, remembering that resting in Christ is how we resist temptation.

So does this mean that we don't do anything beyond remembering a few verses? Is there anything required of us since Jesus has already made us holy through His sacrifice on the cross? And if the victory has already been won and sin has been defeated, why does temptation keep assaulting us, and often times winning?

I have talked to thousands of young men who get frustrated at their inability to stand up under the sexual temptations they face daily, because they believe they have victory in Christ, but in their daily lives they feel weak and defeated. They try to rely on the strength of the Holy Spirit. They pray and fast, join an accountability group, and use Internet filtering services, but they get frustrated when they fail. They often keep giving in to the same temptations. Then they feel guilt and shame if they look at porn, hook up, or can't control their thoughts. I admit that I've felt the same way. Is there a way forward through these struggles?

The Battle Plan

The great British pastor C. H. Spurgeon once said that even though sinful thoughts may rise, they must not reign. In other words, you'll have some sinful thoughts, but you don't have to let them take over your mind or your life. It is not a sin to be tempted, because even Jesus was tempted. We can resist temptation before it turns into sin. I want to suggest a plan of attack that stands on the victory of Christ over sin while simultaneously moving forward based on your decision to fight temptation. When you want to win over temptation, here are three things that can help

HATE IT. STARVE IT. OUTSMART IT.

Hate it.

Take a position of absolute hatred toward sin. Decide you won't tolerate wrongdoing. Get angry about the way sin offends God. Despise the negative ways sin hurts you and your body. Move away from self-pity and take the offensive. Categorize sin and temptation along with things like Ebola and Bird Flu—hate and avoid them! This is the only attitude that works in the fight against temptation. Holiness happens when you hate sin.

Starve it.

Every enemy loses when the food supply is cut off. The French general Napoleon Bonaparte said, "An army marches on its stomach."[3] To defeat temptation, quit feeding it. This may mean ending a relationship, putting filters on your computer, getting rid of the Internet on your phone, staying off social media, or avoiding parties and places where you know you'll meet people that want to hook up. Be ruthless and starve the appetite for sexual sin. The longer you starve it, the weaker it becomes.

Outsmart it.

Get out ahead of your enemy by predicting the ways you'll be tempted before you're tempted. Devise a plan. Don't allow yourself to be blindsided. Decide you'll never be alone with some someone that you want to mess around with. Ask friends to hold you accountable in areas you struggle with. Choose to only go on group dates for a season. Don't have a TV or computer in your room. Turn off your smartphone every night an hour before bed. Read reviews of movies before you buy a ticket to make sure there's no nudity, sex, or even a hint of sexual images that will stick in your brain. Don't be dumb; outsmart the sin. The basis for this approach comes from the Old Testament. I've gone back to this passage consistently in my own struggle against temptation. Notice the words in italics.

> How I love Your instruction! It is my meditation all day long. Your commands make me *wiser* than my enemies, for they are always with me. I have more *insight* than all my teachers because Your decrees are my meditation. I *understand* more than the elders because I obey your precepts. I have *kept* my *feet* from every evil path to follow Your word. I have not turned from Your judgments, for You Yourself have instructed me. How sweet Your word is to my taste—sweeter than honey in my mouth. I gain

understanding from Your precepts; therefore I *hate*
every false way. (Ps. 119:97-104, emphasis mine)

The psalmist hates sin. The last line plainly states that he
hates "every false way." I know *hate* is a strong word. You may
not feel comfortable with using the word *hate* because you
were taught to never hate anyone. But this is not about hating
a person! This is about hating what God hates, and God hates
sin. We should hate every "false way" that leads us away from
intimacy with God. Is it wrong to hate cancer, rape, or racism?
Of course not. We know intuitively it's good to hate bad things.
Cancer, rape, and racism are terrible, wicked things, but sin is
more devastating than all of these, because sin is the root cause
of all such things. Begin now to hate sin, because sinful practices
are harmful and destructive like cancer. Hating sin is the first
step in resisting temptation. God hates sin because He is holy
and because He loves you, and sin hurts you, so He hates it. We
should, too.

The psalmist starves sin. He says that he has "kept [his] feet
from every evil path." He decided that he would not feed any evil
desire. He would not walk in the path that led to wicked places. He
would avoid things and people that led to sinful outcomes. Instead
of moving toward temptation, he moved away from it by going a
different direction. He pursued something better—intimacy with
God. This can be our model for starving our appetite for sexual
sin. It's not enough to cut off the food supply because you will still
be hungry for nourishment. Instead of feasting on sin, we feast
on God. We read His Word, meditate on His wisdom, grow closer
to Christ through worship, and get stronger in community. Our
faith grows stronger when we feed it. Lust and temptation grow
weaker as we starve them and keep our feet from every evil path.

The psalmist outsmarts sin. He says that God's commands make him "wiser than [his] enemies," that he has "more insight" than his teachers, and that he understands "more than the elders" because he obeys God's precepts. Submitting to God's Word is the only way we can outsmart sin with insight and wisdom. We know we can't win on our own. The good news is that we don't have to devise some complex plan full of intricate tricks to resist temptation. The way we outsmart temptation is to read, know, and obey the Bible. Jesus did this. When Satan tempted Him to sin, Jesus relied on the simplicity of Scripture by quoting it in the moment of His weakness. And it worked. Jesus is Lord and He calls the shots. If we trust Him, we will do what He says. And if we want to know what He says, we find it in His Word. We outsmart temptation by submitting to God and applying the wisdom of Scripture.

Adopt and Adapt

You can *adopt* this battle plan and *adapt* it to your particular situation. Though each of us struggles with sin and temptation, those desires look very different in each individual life, ranging from overcoming our past to same sex attraction to a strong appetite for porn. Your issue may be jealousy, or insecurity, or anger, or the overpowering pull on your heart to go back to an old flame whenever you feel lonely or depressed. Adapt your strategy according to the enemy. Jesus did this masterfully when tempted by Satan. We can learn from the Master.

When Jesus died on the cross, He said, "It is finished" (John 19:30). This didn't mean that He was finished. His words meant that the mission He came to accomplish was completed. He was announcing the kingdom of God in all its power. We have a place in His kingdom, which is infinitely more satisfying than the quick pleasure of giving into sin.

We're not fighting this battle alone. The victory is already ours. We're not fighting *for* victory. We're fighting *from* victory. And understanding this simple truth is a game changer.

FAITHFUL AND FREE

You've never gone to war with the British. Why would you? They are close allies with the United States! But things weren't always this way. Nearly 250 years ago, our ancestors were living under the rule of the British Empire. They declared their independence from England and launched the Revolutionary War. The Americans won and we became a free people. Though we never fought in that war, we enjoy the freedoms our ancestors won for us because they fought a war that was for us. We have freedom because of their sacrifice.

Like our ancestors who fought for our freedom long before we were ever born, Jesus died for our freedom thousands of years before we ever faced temptation. He faced an opponent that we could never defeat, but through His sacrifice on the cross, He triumphed over all enemies—including sexual sin and temptation. We enjoy the benefits of His victory. This is the good news of the gospel. Because He was faithful, we are free—free to resist temptation and not be enslaved to sin. Holiness restrains sinful desires and temptation. It liberates us to live a full life with joy and hope in the power of the gospel to change us. As we grow in holiness, God will use our witness as a testimony to change others.

QUESTIONS FOR DISCUSSION

1. What comes to mind when you hear the word "holiness"? How does that compare with the teaching on holiness in this chapter?

2. What is dangerous about pursuing holiness from a performance perspective?

3. What changes when you pursue holiness from your position in Christ?

4. How has Christ saved us from slavery to sin? How aware are you of this reality on a daily basis. How could you grow in your awareness?

5. Of the first steps of growing in holiness that Clayton mentioned (submission, direction, instruction, action, and destination), which is the most difficult for you?

6. Do you have a battle plan for pursuing holiness? If not, what is one step you will take this week in order to intentionally pursue Christ?

7. In what areas of your life are you most tempted to give into sin? Why?

8. What steps could you take to hate, starve, and outsmart sin this week?

9. Who do you know that you could confess sin to and seek accountability from?

10. Pray for the strength and courage necessary to confess sin to and seek accountability from an older brother in Christ this week.

CHAPTER 5

MISSION

ABOUT THE AUTHOR

Mike Taylor *serves as the Director of UK-USA Ministries and Tees Valley Youth for Christ. He also serves as the lead pastor of The Vine Church Teesside. He and his wife, Kookie, have been married for nearly 33 years and they have four children. Mike and Kookie live in Stockton on Tees in the United Kingdom. Prior to living and serving in England, Mike was a youth pastor in the United States for 31 years. You can find out more about Mike and the ministry he leads at www.uk-usaministries.com.*

A few years ago, my youngest son had a few unexpected days off from school so we headed off on a camping and canoeing trip to the Buffalo River in Northwest Arkansas. As we made our way up from Houston, Texas to Fayetteville, Arkansas we talked about everything we wanted to see and do while we were out adventuring in the wilderness. A quick phone call to a friend at the Buffalo Outdoor Center revealed that the river was closed due to all the recent rain. Our hopes and dreams of paddling together were swallowed up with a swollen river that had exceeded its banks and was over the bridge in Ponca. As I hung up the phone my friend said, "Check back in the morning. You know how quickly things change on this river. Maybe we can get you on mid morning tomorrow." So with that, we continued on through Oklahoma and soon arrived at my mom's house in Fayetteville. I grew up climbing all through the Buffalo National Forest and paddling the Buffalo River. I was so excited to get Hayden out on the river and soak up some of God's amazing creation together.

Upon arriving at "Grammer's," I told her of my conversation with my friend concerning the river and she said rather flippantly, "Well, if you guys get to go I might want to join you!" I laughed out loud and headed off to get ready for bed. Later that night as I thought about our drive up and all that we wanted to do together, I was disappointed about the river being closed, but so hopeful that we could go in the morning. Then it dawned on me that I might just be crazy. Who takes their eleven-year-old son and his seventy-five-year-old mother on a raging torrent flood stage river? With that I dozed off to sleep.

When I woke up, I checked on the water levels and discovered they dropped just enough that it would be open by the time we arrived. I was so excited about the prospect of canoeing that I bounded out of bed and went to have breakfast, only to discover that my mom was already packing to join us in our adventure. I proceeded to try and talk her out of it as I knew the river would be raging and very cold. She reminded me that she had paddled that river plenty of times and she would be fine. I woke Hayden and we headed off on our adventure together.

As we drove I must admit I was giddy, like a kid on Christmas Eve. As we descended down into the Buffalo National Forest to the river below, I was overwhelmed with the beauty of the day and the adventure ahead. When I caught my first glimpse of the river, my heart started pounding. It was really moving. I had only paddled the river in this state on a few occasions. At the launch point, the volume of the river rushing below the bridge struck me. Then I heard Hayden proclaim, "I am *not* going on *that* river." Ignoring his fear-filled comment, I continued over to the guys from the Buffalo Outdoor Center who were unloading our canoe. Again when we reached the edge of the river, Hayden said, "There is no way I am going to go on this river."

While I loaded our gear into the canoe, I reminded him that I had done this many times. He interrupted, "Yeah, but not with me and not when it looks like this!" Grammer chimed in, "Hayden, it will be fine. Your dad never tips over!" I silently thought, "Go Grammer"; however, in the back of my mind I was thinking: *There are no guarantees today!* I placed my hands on either side of Hayden's face and looked into his eyes. In all seriousness I asked, "Do you trust me?" He said, "Yes...but I am *not* going on that river." Finally, after several minutes of persuasion I got him to the edge of the raging river, off the bank, and into the canoe.

With Grammer in the front of the canoe and Hayden perched proudly in the middle, we took off.

It was a beautiful spring morning in the Ozarks. We were hemmed in on either side of the river by newly budding, bright green trees. Multicolored sandstone and limestone bluffs towered above the trees. The canopy above us was a brilliant blue, cloudless sky. For just a few minutes I relaxed and settled into the back of the canoe. I knew that the top part of the river was the easiest to navigate, but big challenges waited ahead. By lunch time we made it to Hemmed-in-Hollow, a towering five-hundred-foot waterfall—the highest of its kind between the Southern Appalachians and the Colorado Rockies.

We stopped to hike to the waterfall, and as we walked we could hear the force of the falls from quite a distance. It was majestic, and I marveled at God's incredible handiwork. In that moment, I was so thankful we decided to get off the bank and into the river. In no time, we were back in our canoe slicing through the river and heading into the most challenging part of our journey. This stretch of the river is where people tend to tip over and even the most experienced paddlers grip the oars a bit tighter. I heard the rapids before I could see them around the river's bend. As we approached the whitewater, I yelled above the roar, "Sit low and hold on!"

We dropped down into the first rapid, and the water crashed over us, pretty much filling our canoe with water. The next dip brought even more water. In a matter of seconds, our canoe was almost full of water. With the first diagonal wave, the canoe began to roll. I felt like time stopped long enough for me to say, "We're going to tip over." Simultaneously I screamed, "Get to the bank!" as we tipped over and went under water.

My first thoughts were about getting Hayden and Grammer to safety. My second thought was that if I didn't catch the canoe, it would wrap around a tree at the next rapids and we would be stuck. So, I did my best Michael Phelps impersonation and frantically freestyled after our canoe. I reached it just as it neared the next rapid. I grabbed the back of the canoe and dug my heels into the gravel and sand of the riverbed. Pressing with all my strength, I wrestled it away from the mouth of the rapids. I pulled it over to the edge of the river and plopped down, exhausted from the struggle. Almost immediately, my thoughts turned to my eleven-year-old son and my seventy-five-year-old mother. I desperately hoped they made it to the bank.

I tried walking along the river's edge to make my way back to them, but couldn't make it through the thick brush. The only way I could reach them was to paddle upstream along the bank. The water was moving so fast in the middle of the river it almost created a backdraft along the edges. As I made my way, I began calling out to them. No response. The river was so loud they couldn't hear me nor I them. I was now not far from where we rolled over. I pulled the canoe up on to the bank and began to walk. As I came around the last protruding part of the bank I could see them in the water precariously clinging to the trunk of a tree. I was relieved that they made it to the bank.

My son was wide-eyed and keyed up. I immediately had this thought: *We are all wired for adventure.* We are all called to leave the comfort of the bank and the edge of the river. We are called to step into the raging torrent of the river of God and experience all that He has for us. We are made for more. We are called to live wide-eyed and keyed up. I will never forget the look on Hayden's face—it became part of our journey together and part of our family's story of faith. Anyone can stay on the sidelines or on the bank of the river. It takes a step of faith to join God in the middle of His roaring, redemptive river. So how do you get there? What needs to happen for you to join God in the river? What are the components that make up a missional life? What does a man on a mission look like?

COMPONENTS OF MISSION

Trust

When you go on mission, you have to trust the One calling you and leading you on that mission. On the bank of the river that day, Hayden had to look beyond the circumstances surrounding him. He had to look past the fear and danger, and look into my eyes and trust me. You and I have to do the same thing every day in our spiritual journey. You have to trust the One calling you. Trust is born out of relationship. Hayden knew I wouldn't willingly put him in danger or cause harm to him, so he could get into the boat and go on the ride of his life.

God asks us to trust Him. He longs for you to trust Him not only in salvation, but also in mission. I think most of us have it backward—we give our lives over to Christ and believe that's the end of the road, the end of our responsibility. But salvation is only the first step, the beginning of the rest of the story God wants to write with your life. We are also called to join God's global mission to redeem the world. To fulfill that call on our lives, we have to trust God. God doesn't promise that the journey will be safe, easy, or free from pain and fear. He does promise that He will go with us. Because of that, we can trust Him. All other components of a life on mission tend to naturally flow out of a deep, abiding trust in God.

Positioning Yourself to Be Used By God

I have often wondered how it is that God chooses to use certain people. Have you ever had that thought? *Why did God choose him? Why is he making such an impact with his life?* I think a lot of that has to do with our usability and availability. Are you positioning yourself to be used by God? Are you doing the things necessary to be an instrument God can use for His glory? Take a look at 2 Timothy 2:20-22.

> Now in a large house there are not only gold and silver bowls, but also those of wood and clay, some for honorable use, some for dishonorable. So if anyone purifies himself from anything dishonorable, he will be a special instrument, set apart, useful to the Master, prepared for every good work. Flee from youthful passions, and pursue righteousness, faith, love, and peace, along with those who call on the Lord from a pure heart.

Part of placing yourself in position to be used by God is living with a pure heart—personal holiness. So, as you look to live your life on mission, are you positioning yourself moment by moment to be used by God? If you have truly given your life to Christ and been born again, then your eternity is sealed and your life is hidden with Christ. When God looks at you He sees His Son and your sin is covered by the blood of Jesus. Your standing before God is sealed for eternity. What happens when we don't feel clean and usable? What happens when our lives are stained by the day to day struggle with sin in our personal lives?

Growing up, I didn't go to church much. I knew about God, but didn't truly have a personal encounter with Him until just after my sixteenth birthday. I trusted in Christ on a wilderness backpacking experience with Young Life out in Colorado. Our time on the trail, hiking in the deep wilderness of the rugged San Juan Mountain Range of the Rockies, was incredibly challenging and demanding. Each day we covered several miles of dry, dusty, and difficult terrain. It was August, and hot dry air burned through to the soles of my feet. Anytime we came to a river we would take our boots off and put our hot, tired, blistered feet in the cool mountain water. The water washing over our feet and legs was so refreshing. This is how we are meant to live—in the presence of God with His river of life coursing through us.

When I gave my life to Christ, I felt like He picked me up off a dry, dusty, and difficult trail and placed me in the cool, refreshing river of God. Still, as most of us go through daily life, sin creeps in. The Enemy throws rocks into the river, disturbing the surface, then lodging underneath, seemingly unnoticed and hidden. If we choose to sin again or not deal with sin, then he keeps throwing rocks. Eventually, you find yourself in a dry riverbed, with a dam of rocks blocking what once was the river of God's power and presence. I think many of us feel like that sometimes, we know we have met the Lord and have given our lives over to Him, and yet we begin to feel lost, dry, unworthy, and unusable.

At some point we felt the full assurance of His presence, but because we have not dealt with our day-to-day sin and wrong attitudes we don't feel His presence so strongly. We stop believing He wants and is able to use us for His gospel and glory. So, how do you position yourself for the glory of God and mission? We must deal with sin in the moment, as it happens. *God, forgive me for my bitterness.* You reach up and remove the stone that blocks your view of God. *God, forgive me for my temper.* Then, you remove another stone. *God, forgive me for my lustful thoughts.* Another stone removed. Before long, you will see the water begin to pass through the pile of stones in front of you. As we deal with our daily sin, the river of God is released to wash over us. Again, you feel God's power. Again, you sense His presence. You begin to feel like you can be used again. I call this *practicing God's presence*, constantly experiencing God's real, abiding presence. You cannot live on mission for God without experiencing God's presence.

If *usability* relates to holiness and a pure heart, *availability* is all about attitude and a servant's spirit. Are you available to God? Are you willing to serve the Lord and others? In Matthew 20:28, Jesus said, "The Son of Man did not come to be served, but to serve, and to give His life as a ransom for many." Does your attitude about serving reflect His heart? The heart of Jesus was to serve others. God in human form came to seek and save the lost, and He did it by laying down His life and serving others. He modeled what mission should look like: Serve.

Mission is a mindset, and our minds need to shift to looking for ways to serve others. I believe that when we serve our friends, family, and community, people will begin to ask why. That question will allow us to point people to Jesus. It will lead to a conversation about how Jesus has radically changed your life. Living on mission means that when you walk into a crowded room, you do not see yourself as the most important person there—your mindset has shifted to that of a servant. You begin to see others the way Jesus sees them. Home, school, work, and friends will all look different when we see them through the lens of God's call on our lives to be servants and live on mission for Him.

I love the "why" question. When I moved from Texas to Teesside nearly five years ago I had so many people ask me why. Why England? Why now? When we arrived in The Tees Valley, every time I opened my mouth people said, "You're not from here. Are you an American?" The questions continue today. When they hear that I am from Texas and moved across the ocean to the Northeast of England they always want to know why and follow that with "You are crazy." This leads to the next component of living on mission—risk.

Risk

In our world today, people look at risk many different ways. So much of our culture chases the buzz or rush that comes from living a risky lifestyle. The problem with chasing the buzz is that it's always a temporal high. It is short lived and creates a craving for the next risky adventure. The desire for the next great moment is one long, unsustainable spiral. What happens when the music stops? Or when the event is over? What happens when that particular exciting adrenaline-filled adventure ends or is filled with unmet expectations? Let's be honest most of our risky behavior is focused on us—our wants and desires.

What if our risk was God-centered? What if our risk was gospel-centered? What if there was a shift from focusing our lives on ourselves to a God-centered life that led to us risking more for God's kingdom? I love this definition of risk: Risk is intentional interaction with uncertainty. When I first read that definition, these words from Hebrews 11:1 came to mind, "Now faith is the assurance of things hoped for, the conviction of things not seen" (ESV). You see, faith and risk have always been woven together. Faith is trusting in something even when you cannot see it. You and I place our faith in something every day. I don't have the understanding of electricity like Thomas Edison, but when I walk into a dark room, the first thing I do is flip on the light switch. I don't know the first thing about cars, but I drive one everyday. I cannot wrap my mind around how you can get a plane that weighs between 150,000 and 900,000 pounds off the ground, but I happily get on board and fly across the Atlantic Ocean. I flip the switch, start my car, and hop on a plane because I have done all those things in the past and know they work. We will reach for those things to use tomorrow, because we know or assume they are going to work when we place our faith in them again today.

How does all this relate to mission and God-centered risk? Having true faith means trusting and believing God even when we cannot see Him. We can start on our journey of biblical faith by trusting Him today, but that faith leads to risking more for Him tomorrow. What are you trusting God for today? In what situations are you depending on Him, because you know if He doesn't act, nothing will happen? I believe God wants to do extraordinary things through you. His heart is to use you as an agent of change in your family. I believe that He can use you to reach your friends for Christ today. He has a great adventure prepared for you. But you have to risk, you have to step out in faith and step into all that He has for you. Most of us never live in that realm of total dependence on God. I believe that when we risk for God, we are driven to a dependency on Him we cannot reach with out risk. Stepping out in faith and risking for God drives us to lean into Him, to totally depend on Him. Our dependence on the Lord leads to an intimacy that only comes from risk. The rush of God's never-ending faithfulness far exceeds the temporal pleasure and adventure this world can give. What are you willing to risk for God's kingdom? Prayerfully decide, and then go for it!

When you step out and go for it, you step in obedience. Obedience is doing what you are told to do, when you are told to do it, with a right heart attitude. If we are honest, most of us tend to push back against being told what to do. You can trace that all the way back to the garden. We would much rather make all our own decisions and do what we think is best for us. God sees things quite differently; He always has our best interest in mind. He has called all of us, if we are followers of Christ, to go. Although often forgotten, the call to "go" is a command. Read Jesus' words in Matthew 28:18-20:

Then Jesus came near and said to them, "All authority has been given to Me in heaven and on earth. Go, therefore, and make disciples of all nations, baptizing them in the name of the Father and of the Son and of the Holy Spirit, teaching them to observe everything I have commanded you. And remember, I am with you always, to the end of the age."

I know you have probably heard the Great Commission many times before; however, I think there are some incredibly life altering statements in these three verses. Jesus spoke with authority (Matt. 7:28-29)—the great commission is a command—when He calls us to go, our obedience is assumed. I don't know what authority to compare this to in your world, but for me it was the head football coach. I was always a bit of a class clown in school and in the locker room. Still, when the head football coach walked into the locker room and said something, everyone stopped, listened, and obeyed. He was only a man, but he carried authority. We did whatever he said.

In this passage, the resurrected Son of God spoke with "all authority" and for some reason we don't stop, listen, and obey. He also instructed us to "go" to "all nations." Often, when I speak to students and share the story God is writing here in the UK, I pray that God will "call out the called" to join us here. I believe we are all called to go. Some are called to go five thousand miles from home, like us, and others are called to stay close, but we are all called to go. For you, it might be five feet across the school corridor, or across the locker room to a teammate. Maybe you will *go* to your home and your community. Jesus commanded us both to go and to make disciples. Now watch this, this is life changing:

When we go, He promises that He will go with us. You want real adventure? Do you want to experience the powerful and watch God do the supernatural? Consider this next verse.

> "But you will receive power when the Holy Spirit has come on you, and you will be My witnesses in Jerusalem, in all Judea and Samaria, and to the ends of the earth." (Acts 1:8)

God's power and God's presence are promised to us as we go! It makes sense that many of us don't ever seem to experience His power and presence, because we are not actively sharing Christ as we go. Adventure, God's power, and God's presence are all tied to going in obedience. We are commanded to share the gospel as we go. As a Christian, life lived on mission is anything but boring or normal. If you want to experience a real life of adventure, I invite you to join God on His global mission and step out in obedience to be a witness of His transforming power in your life. Will you take God at His word? It is time to get off the riverbank and experience His power moving through you as you obey His call on your life to go.

Remember, obedience is costly. If you live on mission, it will indeed cost you something. God is well acquainted with sacrifice. He willingly sacrificed His one and only Son to pay the price for our sins. It is because of the love of Christ and the ultimate sacrifice He paid on the cross that we are compelled to carry that message to others. Read 2 Corinthians 5:14-21 to learn about the motivation behind our mission.

> For Christ's love compels us, since we have reached this conclusion: If One died for all, then all died.

And He died for all so that those who live should no longer live for themselves, but for the One who died for them and was raised. From now on, then, we do not know anyone in a purely human way. Even if we have known Christ in a purely human way, yet now we no longer know Him in this way. Therefore, if anyone is in Christ, he is a new creation; old things have passed away, and look, new things have come. Everything is from God, who reconciled us to Himself through Christ and gave us the ministry of reconciliation: That is, in Christ, God was reconciling the world to Himself, not counting their trespasses against them, and He has committed the message of reconciliation to us. Therefore, we are ambassadors for Christ, certain that God is appealing through us. We plead on Christ's behalf, "Be reconciled to God." He made the One who did not know sin to be sin for us, so that we might become the righteousness of God in Him.

Living on mission, whether it is across oceans or across the street, always comes with a price tag. It is imperative that you understand the cost of discipleship. Jesus laid down His life and asked us to follow Him. Doesn't it make sense, then, that being a disciple will cost you your life? What does that look like? It doesn't necessarily mean you will physically have to die because of your faith, but it does mean that you will have to die to your self. It means that the way you live looks different to a watching world. Your attitude, words, and actions will all look different. Obedience is costly.

Perseverance

Another important component of living your life on mission is to keep going. Too many people start strong, but fizzle out before the finish line. Trust me, I know it is hard to live out your faith. It is hard to live on mission. It is hard to persevere. Honestly, if it was easy, anybody could do it and we wouldn't need the Lord. There are times I feel like giving up, but on those days I lean into the strength and faithfulness of God. Finish what you start, and finish well.

Gospel Dream

The final component to living a life on mission is to have a gospel dream. My favorite place here in the Tees Valley is Roseberry Topping. It is an iconic rock with a rugged face that juts out from the edge of the North Yorkshire Moors. It is the tallest place in Teesside, and I love it up there because you can see every part of the Tees Valley from that vantage point. Each year, I take the people who come to serve Northeast England on short term mission trips to Roseberry Topping. I read from Ezekiel 37 and share with them the gospel dream we have for this place and for the United Kingdom. The United Kingdom once was the brightest candle that burned for the gospel and sent missionaries all over the world, chasing a gospel dream. Now, it is dry and the church has grown cold and ineffective. Today, less than 3 percent have a personal relationship with Christ. We read Ezekiel 37:1-3 when we reach Roseberry Topping:

> The hand of the LORD was on me, and He brought me out by His Spirit and set me down in the middle of the valley; it was full of bones. He led me all around them. There were a great many of them

on the surface of the valley, and they were very dry. Then He said to me, "Son of man, can these bones live?"

I replied, "Lord God, only You know."

I love the fact that God spoke to Ezekiel and asked him if the dry bones could live again. God was calling Ezekiel *into* faith, to trust God for the unexplainable, and to dare to dream that God could do something no one expects or believes could ever happen. This is life from death—a valley in despair to an army of hope rising up. I believe God is calling you into faith, to dare to dream that God could do something incredible and unexplainable in and through you. To live on mission, I believe you have to have a God-sized dream in your heart. Our dream is that God would once again breathe life into this place, reviving the church and awakening the lost to salvation in Jesus Christ.

That is our dream and it fuels us. It is a dream that keeps us on our knees, totally dependent on the Lord for His provision and power. That is our gospel dream for the Tees Valley and across the United Kingdom. I believe God has a dream for you. I believe He has an incredible adventure planned your life. You have to trust Him. You have to listen and be aware of His leading. You have to be willing to risk and to walk in obedience. He is calling you into adventure on mission, but you have to walk with integrity and a pure heart. He is holding you in His hands, looking into your eyes, and asking you if you trust Him enough to get off the bank and step into the roaring river of adventure with Him. Will you chase a gospel dream?

QUESTIONS FOR DISCUSSION

1. Mike said, "We are all wired for adventure." How have you experienced this? What is the connection between our wiring and the mission God has given us?

2. Trust is born out of relationship. How is trust essential to mission? How can we grow to trust God more deeply?

3. Read 2 Timothy 2:20-22. What are some practical ways you might position yourself to be used by God?

4. What selfish attitudes are holding you back from faithfully engaging in the mission of God? What step will you take to overcome these attitudes this week?

5. How has Jesus served you? What can we learn from his example in terms of how we live on mission?

6. How does our culture tend to avoid or try to guard against risk? How does this run contrary to Christ's call to mission? What might God be calling you to risk for the sake of mission?

7. How does risk deepen our dependence on God? Have you experienced this? How so?

8. Read 2 Corinthians 5:14-21. What might obedience to God cost you? Why are the sacrifices we make for the sake of the mission of God ultimately worth it?

9. When are you most tempted to disengage from the mission God has given us of making disciples? How can we help one another persevere in this mission?

10. What does it look like to have a "gospel dream"? How can we cultivate such a dream for our schools, our teams, or our communities?

CHAPTER 6

LEADERSHIP

ABOUT THE AUTHOR

Ben Trueblood *serves as the Director of Student Ministry for LifeWay Christian Resources and has served the local church as a student pastor for fourteen years. In addition to his role at LifeWay, Ben is involved in training, consulting, and speaking to student ministries throughout the United States. Ben and his wife, Kristin, have four young children and reside in Nashville, Tennessee.*

THE CASE FOR LEADERSHIP

When you hear the word *leadership* what comes to mind? As someone who grew up in church, leadership simply meant I was at church all the time. I attended every camp, every retreat, and every Wednesday night and Sunday morning. I'm sure I missed a few activities, but I don't remember missing often. Maybe your definition of leadership is much like mine. So, let me clear this up for you: Just being at church all the time isn't leadership, and if that's all you're doing then you're not a leader. I wasn't either.

Dr. Jay Strack is a man I've looked up to for over a decade. He has profoundly influenced my own life and the lives of thousands of others throughout his lifetime as an evangelist, advisor and consultant, and now as the President of Student Leadership University. When speaking to groups of young men, he always makes the statement: "It's time for the little boy to sit down and the man to stand up." Reading this book is that moment for you. As a young man, the time for living as a little boy is over, and it's now time to begin living as a man. Essentially, that is the theme of this entire book: getting to the bottom of what God expects of you as you make this transition from little boy to man. The sad news is that few make this transition aside from the natural changes that occur. Becoming a man has far less to do with age and biology than with how you live your life. I've met plenty of "men" at the age of 35 who still act like little boys. Yet, as a student pastor, I've seen plenty of students undertake the responsibility of what it means to be a man of God and live with a level of maturity far beyond their years. I'm convinced one of the reasons many guys don't make this transition is a failed understanding of leadership.

By this point I hope you're asking yourself what the true definition of leadership is. Dr. John Maxwell has defined the concept by saying, "Leadership is influence—nothing more, nothing less."[1] There are many definitions of leadership, but I think this one fits best because of the spiritual implications it carries. As a young man, leadership is something you should desire on some level, but as a Christian, leadership is a calling God has placed on your life. You are designed to be an influencer. You are designed to make a difference. More specifically, you are designed to have an influence and make a difference for Jesus and the gospel. Let's go to God's Word to see what it looks like to live a life of influence.

> "You are the salt of the earth. But if the salt should lose its taste, how can it be made salty? It's no longer good for anything but to be thrown out and trampled on by men.

> "You are the light of the world. A city situated on a hill cannot be hidden. No one lights a lamp and puts it under a basket, but rather on a lampstand, and it gives light for all who are in the house. In the same way, let your light shine before men, so that they may see your good works and give glory to your Father in heaven." (Matt. 5:13-16)

In this passage Jesus used three pictures to illustrate the influence believers should have in the world. Jesus said we are the salt of the earth, a city on a hill, and a lamp placed on a lampstand. All three of these pictures show us how believers are called to live out their faith boldly, in public—we are not called to hide what we know. At some point in life, many Christians begin to believe that their faith is something that can and should be kept private. This is especially true for men. The culture will tell you your Christian faith should be kept quiet, and you're considered intolerant of others if you speak out about what you believe. Don't fall into this trap. Jesus calls you to be an active influence in the world. This is true regardless of personality type, perceived level of awkwardness, and giftedness—Jesus made no mention of an age qualification for ministry. Bottom line: Your life is designed to influence others for the sake of the gospel. You are designed for leadership. Let's take a closer look at the three pictures in Matthew 5 to see how this happens.

Salt

Salt has two main purposes: flavoring and preserving. You're probably familiar with the use of salt for adding flavor, but the preserving aspect of salt is less familiar to us today. Coating meat in salt keeps the meat from rotting as quickly. Interestingly, the purer the salt is, the longer it will last and fulfill its purpose. The opposite is also true. Salt that contains a lot of impurities deteriorates quickly, becoming useless in its function of flavoring and preserving. We can learn a couple of things here. First, "as salt preserves and brings out the best flavor of food, believers should influence others positively."[2] As you lead, you influence people, and you should bring out the best in them. Any experience with you at your school, your neighborhood, or in your house should be positive and point people to Jesus. The world is so full of negativity—gossip, fighting, bullying, and tearing each other down—that when a believer chooses to live this "salty" life he can make an immediate impact. Second, impurity in our lives will keep us from having a "salty" influence on others. Simply put, "to make a difference in the world, you have to be different from the world."[3] Jesus has given you His perfect life, made you holy, and sent the Holy Spirit to dwell in you and help you live according to His way. The next step is to actually live God's way. Being a leader and influencing people for the sake of the gospel happens in conjunction with a life of holiness.

A light on a lampstand

This is a combination of what Jesus said in verses 14 and 15. The basic idea is the same idea expressed through the salt illustration. Jesus used a different picture here to drive home the importance of His point. Light separates the darkness, invades the darkness, and drives the darkness out. The darkest place I have ever been is the back of a cave in Devil's Den State Park near Northwest Arkansas, where I grew up. All caves, if you walk back far enough, will plunge into complete darkness. However, this was the first time I experienced such intense darkness. We were in the cave for about an hour when our guide decided to ask all of us turn off our headlamps. It was so dark that you could not see your hand in front of your face. I couldn't see anything but blackness, and there was a thickness to this blackness that was deeply unsettling. After a few minutes, our guide told us to power on our headlamps, and in that split second the darkness fled. The retreating darkness left even the furthest corners and shadows of the rock, and we were once again standing in the light. That is what light does—it forces out the darkness. And this is what believers are called to do, as well. Jesus said, "You are the light of the world," (Matt. 5:14a). This world is a very dark place, but when you are in a dark place and someone turns on a light, you can't help noticing the light. A life of influence means being and sharing that light; it means you will live your faith openly for everyone to see.

Before we move on, there are a few more things you should know about being a light. First, if you want to be a light, then you must live in the light. Your attitudes, actions, and behaviors should reveal that Jesus lives in you. Look at another one of Jesus' statements about light: "I am the light of the world. Anyone who follows Me will never walk in the darkness but will have the light of life" (John 8:12b). Second, as you "walk in the light," you reveal who Jesus is to the people around you. You are His representative here on earth. Your light should always point to the greater Light (John 8:12), not to yourself. The point isn't to show what a good Christian or leader you are. We have no shot at being good outside of Jesus. It is only through Him, His power, and His perfect life that we can live as the lights He calls us to be. Third, just as the lamp in Matthew 5 gives light to everyone in the house you are to spread the light of Christ to every person you come in contact with. Sometimes, this will mean sharing the gospel with them, or telling your story, and at times it may mean showing them the love of Christ by serving them in some way. Spreading God's light could also be a combination of all of the above. Let me also clear up a misunderstanding for you about being the light: Just living a life that honors God and serving people doesn't encompass all that it means to be a light and an influencer. You must use your words. True leaders will lead both by example and through their words.

A city on a hill

Imagine for a moment that you're staring up at a castle built on top of a hill. You see the high walls, the guards stationed with bows, the flags rippling in the wind, and the narrow path leading up to the sturdy wooden gates. Cities during Jesus' time were built on high ground for a reason. The high ground was easier to defend and could be seen for miles by those who looked to the city for protection. A city like this would give comfort to people as they worked and lived on the land below. The city was a silent and strong influence to everyone nearby.

Sometimes when we talk about leadership in relation to young men, the image you see is a general who stands at the front of an army bellowing out orders. The picture of a leader this culture gives often portrays leaders as loud, obnoxious, and aggressive. I want you to know that leadership isn't always loud. Sometimes it may be, but there's also a silent and strong leadership men need to embrace. You don't always have to yell and stand in the front of a group to be a leader or make your beliefs known. Leadership isn't always loud, but it always influences.

Leadership and the Gospel

Jesus Himself is the perfect example of this kind of leader. He knew when to be loud, when to be stern and direct with instruction, and when to subtly love and serve people. As you grow in experience leading and seeking to influence people, you will come to understand that leadership is about serving other people more than giving direction. This is the essence of the gospel: Jesus ultimately came not "to be served, but to serve" (Matt. 20:28). If anyone ever deserved to be served, it would be Jesus. He is the Son of God, absolutely perfect in life and in His attributes, and is the Creator of all that has been made. Colossians 1:15-23 explained in detail the supremacy of Christ, and in that supremacy He above all else deserves to be served. Still, He came to earth as a servant. Matthew went on to say Jesus came to give His life as a ransom for many. Let's take a look at the entire verse and meditate on its truth:

> Just as the Son of Man did not come to be served, but to serve, and to give His life—a ransom for many. (Matt. 20:28)

This statement from Jesus followed an argument between the disciples about who would have the seat of honor next to Him in heaven. They wanted to know who was the best. Jesus responded to them by saying, "whoever wants to be the greatest among you must be your servant" (Matt. 20:26), which was made even more powerful by the declaration that Jesus Himself came to serve. However, Jesus didn't only come to serve; He also came to give His life as a ransom for us. It is important for you to understand the theological concept of Jesus' life as a ransom. A ransom is money that is paid in order to free someone who has been captured.[4] You and I are immediately captured by sin when we enter this world. The Bible describes our captivity different ways, such as dead in sin, slaves to sin, and chained in sin. Death is the price that we must pay because of our sin. However, Jesus paid this price, or ransom, for our sin so we could be free. He was our substitute. The price for sin was too high for us to pay on our own, so Jesus willingly laid His life down to pay the price in our place. He was the greatest servant of all because He served God in obedience even when it cost Him His life, while serving unworthy humanity through His substitutionary death. It may be easy to serve those whom we respect, love, or hold a place of honor. It takes a completely different kind of strength to serve those who we would see as unworthy or unimportant. According to Paul, believers should carry the same attitude that Jesus carried all the way to the cross.

> Have this attitude in yourselves which was also in Christ Jesus, who, although He existed in the form of God, did not regard equality with God a thing to be grasped, but emptied Himself, taking the form of a bond-servant, and being made in the likeness of men. Being found in appearance as a man, He humbled Himself by becoming obedient to the point of death, even death on a cross. (Phil. 2:5-8, NASB)

Leadership is influence and servanthood. Leadership doesn't begin on the stage. True leadership begins at people's feet. First and foremost "leadership begins at the feet of Jesus."[5] Submitting yourself to Jesus' leadership means your life is lived for Him, period. Your attitudes are for Him. Your talents are for Him. Your extra-curricular activities are for Him. Who you date and the way you treat your parents are for Him. This is one of those moments we talked about earlier, in which the little boy sits down and the man stands up. Culture will tell you that a true man, a leader bows his head for no one. Culture will tell you that a true man will squash and climb over anything and anyone make it to his destination. However, the Bible teaches that a leader should grab a towel and some water and begin washing people's feet. If that sounds weird to you turn to John 13:1-17 and read the account of Jesus washing the disciples' feet. In that day, washing feet was a necessary, yet disgusting task reserved for the lowliest of servants. Here, Jesus humbled Himself to this lowly place in order to serve His disciples. In our everyday lives, being a leader means we look for opportunities to serve people, even in ways that could be seen as demeaning or embarrassing. Being a leader doesn't mean you strive to be first; it means you place yourself in a position to serve as many people as you can, and by doing so you reveal the light of Christ.

The Leadership Responsibility

As you can probably tell by now, leadership involves people—the people you lead, the people who mentor you and offer you advice, and the people who will one day take over your leadership role. True leadership involves other people. Because of this I want you to focus on two biblical examples that will show the importance of other people in your life as a leader. The first is from the life of Moses. Many consider Moses to be one of the greatest leaders in the Bible. Yes, he certainly had some flaws, but God still used Him in an incredible way. In fact, throughout Scripture you will see God's amazing forgiveness and restoration played out in the way He often uses flawed people to accomplish His task. This is important for us to realize because we are also incredibly flawed as a result of our sin. Take comfort in knowing that God can and still wants to use you.

Let's get back to Moses. If you study his life you will see that he made sure to keep one specific person close to him most of the time as he led the people of Israel. This person was Joshua. When Moses did something significant or had an important task to complete, Joshua was right there learning, listening, or performing the task that Moses needed. It is clear from this relationship that Moses was teaching Joshua how to lead. He was mentoring Joshua, making sure the people would have a well-trained, God-honoring leader to take his place when he was gone.

As a growing leader, you need to find a person who will be like Moses for you. A key relationship in the life of a leader at any age is a person who will mentor and teach him how to be a God-honoring leader. Consider who that person is in your own life. You also need to be like Moses for someone else. Yes, even as a teenager there needs to be a person, or small group of people, you are mentoring. The biblical term for this is discipleship. You don't have to know everything to be able to disciple someone else. If you are a high school student, find a guy who's in middle school to spend time with and share the things you are learning. Through these relationships, you will find that your influence will begin to expand past the lives of that individual or small group and into the lives of their friends as well.

If you don't have these relationships, the damage can be catastrophic. This was exactly the case with Moses and Joshua. Once Joshua took over the leadership of the people of Israel, there's no evidence of Joshua mentoring someone else to take his place as Moses did for him. Joshua was able to accomplish incredible things for God, but didn't train anyone else. He didn't bring another group of people alongside him, and it cost the people of Israel dearly. Within one generation's time from Joshua's death the people had forgotten the works God did in their past. Leadership is influence, servanthood, and leaving a legacy. Make sure that when you are gone there are people who will continue the task.

Our second biblical example is Rehoboam, the son of King Solomon. In 1 Kings 12, King Solomon had died and Rehoboam took over leadership of the Southern Kingdom of Israel. The people of Israel came to King Rehoboam and shared how his father had made their lives difficult. They told Rehoboam if he lightened their load, then they would serve him and be his people. Rehoboam told the people he would think about their request and instructed them to come back to him in three days. Here is where we find our second principle of leadership. During these three days Rehoboam sought out advice from two groups of people: the elders who had served his father and the young men he grew up with. The advice of the elders was to serve the people and speak kind words them. His friends' advice was to treat them more harshly than his father and to beat them into submission. Rehoboam chose to listen to his friends, and it eventually cost him the kingdom.

A leader listens to the right voices. Have you ever heard the statement, "You can't expect to fly like an eagle when you are hanging out with a bunch of turkeys"? Here's a reality for you: You will be like the people you spend most of your time with. If you hang out with guys who live for Jesus, serve people, and desire leadership then you will likely also become a successful leader. If you spend time with guys who are heading in the opposite direction, then you will never be able to reach the leadership potential inside of you. This is an area where I've seen young men fail time and again. Your friends really do determine your path and your destination. If you want your destination to be a life of influence for Jesus and the gospel, then you will choose your friends based on that destination.

The Leadership Vacuum

There is a shortage of young men in student ministries who are willing to stand up and be people of influence. This is not the way our lives are meant to be. God designed you to be a person of influence. He has purposed for you to be salt, light, a city on a hill. He has placed His Spirit in you to give you the strength needed to be all those things. Yet, young men fail to respond to God's call to step up. This is your opportunity to take a different path than the majority. This is your chance to respond to God's call to be an influencer in your world. What's holding you back?

For some of you, your sin is holding you back. There's something that you've kept to yourself and you think it disqualifies you from being a leader. Don't allow the enemy to feed you that lie. If you are struggling with this, then check out Colossians 2:14 and what it says about God's forgiveness in your life:

> He erased the certificate of debt, with its obligations, that was against us and opposed to us, and has taken it out of the way by nailing it to the cross.

God's forgiveness is complete and final. He has canceled your debt of sin and the guilt that goes along with it. One of the greatest tactics of the Enemy is convincing someone to be controlled by guilt over sin that has already been forgiven. If your sin is holding you back from being a leader, confess it, repent of it, and move forward in the forgiveness that God has already given you.

Some of you may be held back by fear. You might think you aren't outgoing or talented enough to be a leader. Remember, leadership isn't talent. Leadership is more than an outgoing personality. Leadership isn't popularity. Leadership is influence, and you can have influence. God has placed you somewhere right now where you can have influence for Him and He has given you everything you need to accomplish that task: He has given you Himself. He is sufficient when talent and ability fail. He is sufficient when nervousness and shyness want to take over. He is living in you; now go live for Him.

Some of you may be held back by pride. You want to be popular. You want to be cool. Your decisions and attitudes are based entirely on what other people think about you, so you're hesitant to step out and be an influence for Jesus. It's hard for you to step up because you aren't sure what it will cost you. Honestly, this is a great thing to consider. I would rather young men truly count the cost of following Jesus than bounce back and forth between living for themselves and living for Jesus. We need to understand that this life isn't about us and it isn't about the people who place labels on us or give approval to us. This life is about God and He has already placed His stamp of approval on you because of the life, death, and resurrection of His Son. Know this, God is the only person you don't have to earn approval from. Jesus earned that for you. Seeking the approval of humanity is a fruitless and depressing endeavor that will never end. If this is the area where you are holding back in your leadership, then it is time to choose to live in the approval that Jesus earned for you. It is time to walk away from what others might think and begin to live the life you are designed to live as a man of God who is an influence for Jesus and the gospel wherever you go.

You might be experiencing all three of these issues or some not even mentioned here. Honestly, you may bounce in and out of these obstacles as you grow in your leadership and as the Enemy attacks you at points along the way. Leadership isn't easy, but it is possible. You have been created for it, called to it, and empowered to accomplish it all by and for the glory of God. The choice is yours. Will you be the leader and man God has purposed you to be?

QUESTIONS FOR DISCUSSION

1. In your own words, define the term leadership.

2. What does it mean to be salt in this world?

3. What does it mean to be light in this world?

4. What are some practical ways you can be salt and light in your school, neighborhood, community, household, and so on?

5. What did Jesus mean when He said, "Whoever wants to be great among you must be your servant"?

6. Name a few leaders God placed in your life to train you as a leader. Thank God for those people and spend some time praying that you will be a good mentor as well.

7. Can you think of someone who would be a good "Joshua" for you?

8. How do the people you hang out with most influence your path and destination as a leader?

9. What needs to change in your group of friends that will help you live a life of influence for Jesus?

10. What is holding you back from living a life of influence for Jesus?

CHAPTER 7

DISCIPLE MAKING

ABOUT THE AUTHOR

Jeff Borton *serves as the Next Generation Pastor at Long Hollow Baptist Church in Hendersonville, Tennessee. Having served in student ministry for 16 years, he is passionate about seeing students know Jesus, being discipled and change the world. In addition to his role at Long Hollow, Jeff enjoys writing, speaking and consulting for student ministry. Jeff and his wife, Jen, have three boys, enjoy trips to the ocean, and love watching Wake Forest football.*

Be a disciple who makes disciples.

Henry was like many other kids in Miami. He grew up in a tough neighborhood and his family had very little money. In his neighborhood, learning life on the streets was the norm. His parents were from another country. Henry was a high school student who didn't have a relationship with God and was looking for fulfillment anywhere he went. He realized girls, parties, and friends didn't seem to fill the emptiness he often felt. He was caught in a vicious cycle that offered no hope and no real answers.

A walk in the park one summer afternoon began a cycle of change in Henry's life. Passing through the neighborhood park as usual, Henry was surrounded by seven guys from a rival neighborhood gang. The encounter left him in the hospital for two weeks and his jaw wired shut for six. With a steady diet of liquid food and lame daytime television, he couldn't help but question the direction of his life.

Shortly after returning to health, Henry began to visit a nearby church his mom and sisters attended. The people were nice and he was learning about the gospel, so he returned each week. Just as life seemed to be improving, he heard some devastating news about a friend—the kind of news nobody wants to receive, but happens all too often in Henry's neighborhood. Henry's friend, Spoon, had been shot and killed. Gathering up his brother and some friends, they made their way to the park where the shooting happened. Sure enough, police tape and officers confirmed what happened before they could even ask. Spoon's last moments were lived between a row of bushes and a wall. A graffiti-themed tribute marks that spot to this day. Henry flew into a tailspin. Suddenly he began to question his own mortality and ask some tough questions about life after death. A few weeks later, Henry gave his life to Jesus. Although slowly at first, his life began to change.

One year later, Henry was invited to join a discipleship group. The student pastor had invited five guys to meet every Wednesday night—digging into Scripture, holding each other accountable, and walking through life together. Wednesday nights were fun and often went past midnight. Food, accountability, and spending time in God's Word became very meaningful to Henry.

Change didn't happen overnight. Growth is a process, and God used discipleship to shape Henry into the man He wanted him to be. Case in point, a few months into discipleship, Henry got "busted." It was normal from time to time, for the guys to hand their cell phones over to their leader. He would look at text messages they sent, websites visited, and so on, to be sure everyone was honoring their commitment to be holy, even on their phones. The leader noticed Henry frantically messing with his phone as he was handing it over. Sure enough, Henry had wiped all texts off of his phone. He had been flirting with a girl, it had gone too far, and he was embarrassed. That was a powerful moment for him—he realized the importance of good accountability in his spiritual life.

Life with Christ took on a whole new meaning for Henry. God's Word came to life for him and shaped the way he viewed the world. His desire for girls and parties began to change. He also began to serve in the student ministry he graduated from. After some time, Henry began to lead a small high school group for freshman guys. As his life was transformed, he began to invest in the lives of others in hopes that God would transform them. All of his relationships changed—He began to want a better, more Christlike relationship with his parents and siblings. Eventually, Henry interned in his church, following the call God placed in his heart to serve in student ministry. God continued to change his heart and his love for discipleship grew.

Today, Henry is a student pastor in Miami. As you look around the church where Henry serves, you will see people in several areas of the church Henry has discipled. And many of those disciples, are discipling someone else. Henry was discipled and now invests his life in others. He is a disciple who makes disciples.

DEFICIENT DISCIPLESHIP

Scripture speaks often about disciples. Too often we limit the term *disciple* to the twelve guys that were with Jesus during His ministry years, but this neglects the importance of being a disciple in our context. We easily call the guys with Jesus disciples, but don't commit ourselves to being called disciples. In some circles, we have no problem calling ourselves Christians. In fact, in some parts of the United States, being a Christian is a cultural norm. For these areas, being a Christian is a descriptive term like every other aspect of a person's life—ball player, student, and chicken-nugget connoisseur—*Christian*. This title, coupled with minimal church attendance, works—*I'm a Christian*.

However, Scripture refers to Christians only three times yet refers to disciples over 250 times.[1] Truthfully, Jesus called us to far more than a title. Jesus never used phrases like, "Call yourself a Christian" or "Be sure to be a good person." Jesus didn't call you to be a good church-goer or youth group member. Instead, we see strong commands and descriptions of the characteristics Jesus considers a disciple to possess.

Then He said to them all, "If anyone wants to come with Me, he must deny himself, take up his cross daily, and follow Me." (Luke 9:23)

"Whoever does not bear his own cross and come after Me cannot be My disciple." (Luke 14:27)

Jesus' words do not sound anything like cultural Christianity. Jesus' description of Christianity doesn't make it seem like a popular thing to do. It sounds painful; sacrificial.

Compare what you hear most people discuss when they talk about being a Christian. For most students, you hear a steady diet of "don't have sex" and "bring your friends to church." But Jesus calls you to more. Jesus isn't looking for a good church-goer, He's looking for students who will take up their crosses, lay down their lives, and follow Him no matter the cost.

Dietrich Bonhoeffer was a theologian who lived during World War II. As a pastor, he fought to destroy the work of Adolf Hitler and disciple Christ-followers. He ultimately gave his life for the cause of Christ. Bonhoeffer had a strong view of discipleship and a clear understanding that how we pursue Jesus is a reflection of our understanding of grace. For example, if we have a poor view of God's grace, we believe that once we have been saved there's no need to pursue God because the most important aspect has taken place. We think we should just try to be good people from this point forward. Bonhoeffer clarified the difference between just being comfortable with the title *Christian* and pursuing the life of a disciple, "The disciple's answer is not spoken confession of faith in Jesus. Instead, it is the obedient deed."[2] Being a disciple is more than acknowledgment; it is a constant pursuit of Jesus.

The life of a disciple is marked not by cultural terms, but by obedience and sacrifice. A disciple pursues intimacy with Christ over the comfort of friends, possessions, or approval from others. Francis Chan, author and speaker, told the story of 21 South Korean missionaries who were captured by Muslims and placed in prison. After being searched, one of the missionaries managed to keep a portion of the Bible and distribute a few pages to each of the other prisoners. Soon after, they gathered the prisoners together and told them they were going to start killing them one by one. Immediately, a few of the group began to argue that they wanted to be first to die—it was an honor to die for the glory of Jesus.

Over a period of time, two of the men were murdered and the other 19 were released. A few months later, Chan interviewed one of the prisoners who shared this story. After some discussion, the missionary and former prisoner confessed that he missed being in the jail cell. As terrible as it was, he said he missed the intimacy and trust with God the cell seemed to foster. The pain, solitude, and misery pointed him to God. Jail forced him to draw near to God in a way he'd never experienced, and he wanted to experience that closeness with God again.[3] Disciples value being close to God more than anything this world can offer—even freedom. Still, you can enjoy closeness with God without being in a Taliban prison.

DEFINING DISCIPLESHIP

In ancient Jewish culture, it was easy to tell who disciples were. The rabbis of the day were priests and teachers who taught young men who would grow to be rabbis one day. An average Jewish young man had basically one of two options: study to be a rabbi or continue in the family business. If a young man wanted to be a rabbi, the process was long and difficult. He would memorize the Pentateuch, the first five books of the Old Testament, by the time he was 11. And that was just the prerequisite. The rabbi would examine the young man's life and see if he thought this young man could carry out the duties of a rabbi. The rabbi would ask himself, "Can he do what I am doing?"

If a young man memorized the correct passages, passed some other tests, and was approved, he would begin to follow the rabbi, learning to do what the rabbi did. In essence, he became a follower of the rabbi. This young rabbi in training would continue to learn, grow, and study in his pursuit of becoming more like the rabbi. His life and actions would be watched closely and if he was approved, he would eventually become a rabbi.

Interestingly, when Jesus called his disciples, Scripture never said they were well educated. It appears these were guys chose to continue in the family business. The disciples weren't the rabbi's apprentices, well spoken, or even popular. Jesus chose fishermen and others to be the ones He poured his life into. This practice of choosing common people to be disciples was counter cultural in Jesus' day. Jesus wasn't looking for the well educated or finely polished, He recruited men who would follow Him with every ounce of their being. And they did.

Jesus took ordinary men and transformed them into world changers. They went from fishermen and tax collectors to apostles, church planters, and martyrs. All but one of the Twelve were killed for their faith. The other, John, was severely persecuted and exiled, left to die on an island. Consider this when you think of your own faith: These men would rather die a brutal death than deny Jesus. Let's live our lives with this kind of passion for our Savior.

MORE THAN JUST INFORMATION

When we see how Jesus led His disciples, it's clear they didn't learn in a classroom setting. Jesus lived life with His disciples. They ate together, went to parties together, and even enjoyed boat rides together. (My favorite kind of discipleship!) In John chapter 15, when Jesus taught on the vine and the branches, they were in a garden. The group was on the way somewhere else when Jesus used the vine as a teaching moment for the Twelve. Jesus taught through real life experiences as He and His disciples walked together.

Too often, discipleship is viewed as a download of information. We mistakenly believe avoiding lost people, going to more Bible studies, and listening to Christian music on repeat are equivalent with being discipled. In reality, we are just getting really good at looking the part. For many students, the Christian life is a cycle of trying to be a good person and spend time with God and being frustrated when life doesn't go as planned. The Christian life is confusing when we view it as a list of do's and don'ts. Jesus never intended for us to live life trying to gain His approval or thinking He would love us more if we stopped sinning. God's idea of relationship is so much greater.

As Jesus spent time with and taught the disciples, their eyes were opened and their lives began to change. Jesus spoke truth into their lives and gave them opportunities to live it out. The men didn't just listen to what Jesus taught, they applied it to their lives and ultimately they were transformed. We are promised that same transformation. Galatians 5:22-24 says, "But the fruit of the Spirit is love, joy, peace, patience, kindness, goodness, faith, gentleness, self-control. Against such things there is no law. Now those who belong to Christ Jesus have crucified the flesh with its passions and desires." As we grow in faith and the knowledge of God, we produce fruit. We grow in our knowledge of God when we learn who He is.

WHY THEOLOGY MATTERS

Theology is the study of God. Studying theology means getting to know God and what He is like. It's impossible to be more like God if you do not know who He is. Understanding sound theology will lead you to a proper knowledge of God. As we grow in knowledge of God, our knowledge impacts how we live. For instance, when we truly grasp the holiness of God, we will want to be more holy. First Peter 1:16 says, "Be holy, I am holy." God calls us to be like Him—an impossible task unless we are devoted to knowing Him.

Don't be afraid of theology or learning deeper truths of God's Word. Alvin Reid, a seminary professor, says, "If students can learn algebra and chemistry, they certainly can learn theology!" It's true! Don't sell yourself short. Don't believe the hype. Don't settle for a surface level understanding of who God is when you can know Him intimately. Experience is important, but it should never replace studying God's Word to know Him more.

Kelly Kapic said it like this, "Theology is not reserved for those in the academy; it is an aspect of thought and conversation for all who live and breathe, who wrestle and fear, who hope and pray."[4] Consider what Scripture says:

> But as for you, continue in what you have learned and firmly believed. You know those who taught you, and you know that from childhood you have known the sacred Scriptures, which are able to give you wisdom for salvation through faith in Christ Jesus. All Scripture is inspired by God and is profitable for teaching, for rebuking, for correcting, for training in righteousness, so that the man of God may be complete, equipped for every good work. (2 Tim. 3:14-17)

Theology matters because what you believe about God determines how you will live your life. An imbalanced or unbiblical view of God has far reaching implications. For instance, if we elevated God's love and acceptance over His justice, we might give up on the doctrines of hell and judgment. Such a view contradicts Jesus' claim to be the only way to heaven (John 14:6). Why would there be only one way if God were only love? It is critical that we look to the Bible and let God speak for Himself as we consider who He is and what He is like. When Scripture is not our primary source for understanding God, we will begin making God in our own image.

Other people only see God as angry and judgmental. They hold signs at funerals, yell at people, and tell others God hates them. They too have a wrong view of God; they haven't studied who He is carefully or humbly enough. Viewing God only as vengeful misses the truth about grace and forgiveness that is central . If you say you love God, then grow in your relationship with Him by studying who He is.

DISCIPLES MAKE DISCIPLES

Discipleship takes intentionality. We don't naturally move toward growing in relationship with God; it requires commitment and discipline. Without these two, we drift toward what is most comfortable. We see the idea of drifting at work all around us.

The ocean is an incredible environment. There's an undiscovered world just under the surface—reefs teeming with life, fish of every color, and strange things you only see on movie screens. While what you see can be exhilarating, what is unseen can be quite dangerous. Ocean currents cause many deaths each year—these seemingly invisible forces pull people away from safety and out to their demise. Some currents pull beach-goers out to sea. Other currents drift divers away from their boats in the open ocean. The person in the water must be vigilant about knowing where he is and where he should be. Carelessness or apathy can change the course of your day very quickly—it can be deadly.

This principle of drifting also occurs in our spiritual lives when we lack discipleship. A sense of who we are and what our lives should look like are formed in a discipleship relationship. What does a disciple do? A quick glance at Western culture provides a mixture of messages about the role of a disciple. Some view the role of a Christian to be defensive: defend yourself from lost people and defend the faith. Others believe it's the obligation of disciples simply to tell others about Jesus. Both of these views have elements of truth, but miss the whole picture.

A disciple should understand the faith and tell others about Jesus, but also must make disciples. Making disciples isn't only leading people to a relationship with Jesus, but also helping them live like Jesus. The responsibility of every Christ follower, every disciple, is to help others grow and experience God in a deeper way. If we are really going to understand what a disciple does, we must be clear on what discipleship means. If you were to ask 10 people what discipleship is, you probably wouldn't hear the same answer twice.

Some believe discipleship is just spending time together. We see this often in student ministry. It's often classified as hanging out, playing video games or sports, maybe even eating those cheese fries covered in delicious bacon. While any investment of time is worthwhile, simply hanging out isn't discipleship. Good relationships can be formed when we hang out, but just hanging out won't necessarily guide us toward a deeper relationship with God. Let's look at what God's Word says about discipleship.

Then Jesus came near and said to them, "All authority has been given to Me in heaven and on earth. Go, therefore, and make disciples of all nations, baptizing them in the name of the Father and of the Son and of the Holy Spirit, teaching them to observe everything I have commanded you. And remember I am with you always, to the end of the age." (Matt. 28:18-20)

These verses reveal some of Jesus' final instructions to His disciples. He gave them a final charge to continue His ministry, carrying out the mission of the Father. He spent time with and equipped the disciples, so it was time for them to start investing in others. Many times people mistakenly interpret these verses as a command to *only* lead people to Jesus. In this interpretation, they miss a large part of the command. The word "go" literally translates to *as you are going,* meaning, as you live your life, be making disciples. Christ calls us to make disciples. To teach others about Him. Instruct them. Raise them up in the faith. Leading others to Christ isn't enough, we have a responsibility to help them grow in their faith. In your day-to-day living as a disciple of Jesus, you should be making other disciples.

Here's a scary thought to consider, especially when Jesus' final command was to go and make disciples: A small percentage of Christians can say they have been discipled. Fewer Christians can say they've discipled someone else. Very few can say they have discipled someone who is discipling someone else.[5]

How can we be okay with this? Look at what the Apostle Paul instructed to his young disciple, Timothy.

You, therefore, my son, be strong in the grace that is in Christ Jesus. And what you have heard from me in the presence of many witnesses, commit to faithful men who will be able to teach others also. (2 Tim. 2:1-2)

Paul laid out a clear discipleship strategy for Timothy to follow. He said, "Take what I taught you and teach someone else." Christians shouldn't have a wealth of information and theology without practically helping someone else walk in the faith. Too often Christians are content with yet another Bible study, Facebook argument, or Instagram meme to puff up their knowledge. This isn't how Timothy was instructed to live and neither were we. From Jesus' instructions to His disciples and Paul's instructions to Timothy, we see that a disciple should be doing two main things: Being discipled and discipling someone else.

I once heard a man, who was almost 60 years old, being asked who was discipling him. He laughed off the question and made a comment about being old enough in the faith that he didn't need anyone discipling him. What a catastrophic thought: "I've arrived spiritually. I don't need to be discipled."

Whether you're 12 or 112, seek to be discipled. You can't encourage someone else to be discipled if you aren't being discipled. Once being discipled becomes part of your routine, it will be easier to continue. Don't ever believe you've reached spiritual maturity and no longer need anyone to speak into your life. Being discipled is key to your spiritual growth, but so is discipling others. Imagine the cumulative impact of your life if you were to start discipling a few people this year and continued that for life. Consider the impact if that number grew each year.

Most Christians like the idea of discipling someone, but have no idea where to start. Here are some practical thoughts on beginning the process of discipleship with other believers.

1. Select two or three people, other guys who want to grow in their relationship with God. Key thought here: Invest in people you know will invest in other people. Build a discipleship group with these people, lasting for eight months to one year. Groups like this are called closed groups, because only those invited can join and they can only join at the start of the group. Why do a closed group? This type of group protects the unity and trust for those involved. Discipleship groups that have revolving doors often have trouble keeping traction.

2. Don't feel pressured to know everything to lead a discipleship group. No one, not even your pastor, knows every detail of the Bible. We all have the Holy Spirit, who will guide and equip us. Read, trust, pray, and lead well.

3. Discipleship should be modeled after Jesus. When we study Jesus' teachings, we notice He didn't teach for behavioral modification; Jesus taught to change the heart. Proverbs 4:23 clarifies how all of our passions and pursuits come from the heart, which should be guarded. In the same way, when your heart is changed, the rest of your life is changed. Jesus didn't just want people to stop sinning; He wanted them to love God so much that they hated sin. His goal was not to change their behavior but to transform their hearts.

Author and pastor Robby Gallaty says there are five key components to a great discipleship group. Using the acronym

MARCS, he lays out a healthy expectation for what these groups should look like.

1. **Missional**. One of the fruits of a healthy group is love and concern for lost people. If people are truly growing in their relationships with God, they should be passionate about what God is passionate about. God loves lost people and so should we.

2. **Accountable**. Everyone in the group must be committed to transparency and honesty about issues in their lives. There must be freedom to ask hard questions and seek restoration together. Accountability in the spiritual disciplines, not just in the area of sin, is extremely important.

3. **Reproducible**. If the group was healthy, then the members of that discipleship group should begin their own group when this one ends. That's why we invest in people who will invest in others. The expectation is that discipleship will continue.

4. **Communal**. Jesus set the example for the importance of relationship. Discipleship is sharing life together. Discipleship is not a program, but sharing life through the lens of God's Word.

5. **Scriptural**. Discipleship must be based around the reading, study, and memorization of God's Word. Book studies are nice, but why not study God's love letter to you? If a guy really wants to get to know a girl, he doesn't ask out her best friend, he asks her out. Don't settle for reading what someone else says about God. Instead, get to know God Himself through personal study of Scripture.[6]

As you grow in manhood and your relationship with God, discipleship must be a priority. I'll never forget my first discipleship experience. I had been a Christian for a few years and wanted to grow in my relationship with God. I hadn't really heard about discipleship, even though I was attending a Christian college and a new believer. The college I was attending was adamant that people accept Jesus as their Savior, yet failed miserably at actually making disciples. Just out of my teenage years, an older Christian friend began to meet with me weekly to walk through Scripture together. This experience was mind blowing. For the first time in my life, I began to really understand why I believed what I said I believed. It was actually beginning to make sense. I loved God; I just needed to see the gospel come to life.

QUESTIONS FOR DISCUSSION

1. In your own words, define the term *disciple*. By your definition, are you a disciple of Christ?

2. Share some examples in Scripture of Jesus actively discipling His followers.

3. Share a few things you have had to give up for your personal relationship with Jesus. Was it difficult to give them up? Why or why not?

4. What keeps you from being discipled? What intimidates you the most about being in a discipleship group?

5. Explain what theology means. Why is theology important? How can learning about God actually help you get to know God?

6. How many of your Christian friends have been discipled? Of that number, how many are discipling someone else? If that number is small or non-existent, why do you think that is?

7. Why is it important that a Christian be discipled and disciple someone else?

8. Why should discipleship be based in God's Word? Why is memorizing Scripture important?

9. How can practicing spiritual disciplines (*reading God's Word, praying, fasting, etc.*) help us know and experience God?

10. Pray and list a few friends that you would be willing to lead in a discipleship group. Approach them, and start your own discipleship group.

SOURCES

CHAPTER 1

1. *Braveheart*, DVD, directed by Mel Gibson (1995; Hollywood, CA: Paramount Pictures, 2000.)

2. "More Information About: William Tyndale," *BBC.com*, accessed March 9, 2016, http://www.bbc.co.uk/history/people/william_tyndale/.

3. Dr. James Strong, *Strong's Greek and Hebrew Dictionary* (Nashville: Thomas Nelson, 2010). Accessed via mywsb.com.

4. Jason S. Carroll, Laura M. Padilla-Walker, Larry J. Nelson, Chad D. Olson, Carolyn McNamara Barry, and Stephanie D. Madsen, "Generation XXX: Pornography Acceptance and Use Among Emerging Adults," *Journal of Adolescent Research 23*, no. 6 (2008), accessed March 23, 2016, http://byuresearch.org/ssrp/research.html.

5. Ana Stutler, "The Connections Between Pornography and Sex Trafficking," *CovenantEyes*, September 7, 2011, http://www.covenanteyes.com/2011/09/07/the-connections-between-pornography-and-sex-trafficking/.

6. "Marriage & Divorce," *American Psychological Association*, accessed March 9, 2016, http://www.apa.org/topics/divorce/.

7. Jennifer Glass, "Red States, Blue States, And Divorce: Understanding The Impact of Conservative Protestantism on Regional Variation in Divorce Rates," *Counsel On Contemporary Families*, January 16, 2014, https://contemporaryfamilies.org/impact-of-conservative-protestantism-on-regional-divorce-rates/

8. Ed Stetzer, "Marriage, Divorce, and the Church: What Do The Stats Say, And Can Marriage Be Happy?" *Christianity Today*, February 14, 2014, http://www.christianitytoday.com/edstetzer/2014/february/marriage-divorce-and-body-of-christ-what-do-stats-say-and-c.html.

CHAPTER 2

1. A. W. Tozer, *The Knowledge of the Holy* (New York: HarperCollins, 1961), 1.

2. C. S. Lewis, *The Weight of Glory* (New York: Harper Collins, 1976), 116.

CHAPTER 4

1. Craig Groeschel, *Chazown* (Multnomah: Colorado Springs, 2010) 151.

2. Andy Stanley, *The Principle of the Path: How to Get from Where You Are to Where You Want to Be* (Nashville: Thomas Nelson, 2008), 14.

3. Martin H. Manser, *The Facts on File Dictionary of Proverbs* (New York: Infobase, 2007), 12.

CHAPTER 6

1. John C. Maxwell, "Leadership Is Influence: Nothing More, Nothing Less," *Christianity Today,* July 2007, http://www.christianitytoday.com/le/2007/july-online-only/090905.html?start=2.

2. Bruce B. Barton, Mark Fackler, Linda K. Taylor, and David R. Veerman, *Life Application Bible Commentary: Matthew* (Carol Stream: Tyndale, 1996), 84.

3. Ibid.

4. "Ransom," *Merriam-Webster.com,* [cited March 17, 2016]. Available from the internet: http://www.merriam-webster.com/dictionary/ransom.

5. Brent Crowe, *Sacred Intent: Maximize the Moments of Your Life* (Franklin: Worthy Publishing, 2015). Accessed via https://books.google.com.

CHAPTER 7

1. Robby Gallaty, "What Is Discipleship?" *Replicate Ministries,* June 10, 2013, http://replicateministries.org/2013/06/10/what-is-discipleship/.

2. Dietrich Bonhoeffer, *Discipleship* (Minneapolis: Fortress Press, 2003), 45.

3. Francis Chan, *Forgotten God: Reversing Our Tragic Neglect of the Holy Spirit* (Colorado Springs: David C. Cook, 2009), 81.

4. Kelly M. Kapic, *A Little Book for New Theologians: Why and How to Study Theology* (Downers Grove: Intervarsity Press, 2012), 15-16.

5. "New Research on The State of Discipleship," *Barna Group,* December 1, 2015, https://www.barna.org/research/leaders-pastors/research-release/new-research-state-of-discipleship#.Vw6O2JMrKi4.

6. Robby Gallaty, *Rediscovering Discipleship: Making Jesus' Final Words Our First Work* (Grand Rapids: Zondervan, 2015), 183-202.

NOTES

NOTES

NOTES

NOTES

NOTES

NOTES

NOTES